GOD
WAS
THERE

Books by Martin Weber include

Wrestling With Reality

Hurt, Healing, and Happy Again

Adventist Hot Potatoes

More Adventist Hot Potatoes

Desecration, Danger, Deliverance

My Tortured Conscience

GOD WAS THERE

TRUE STORIES OF A POLICE CHAPLAIN

Martin Weber

Pacific Press® Publishing Association
Nampa, Idaho
Oshawa, Ontario, Canada
www.pacificpress.com

Cover design by Steve Lanto
Cover design resources from iStockphoto.com
Inside design by Aaron Troia

You can obtain additional copies of this book by calling toll-free 1-800-765-6955 or by visiting http://www.adventistbookcenter.com.

Unless otherwise noted, Scripture quotations are from the RSV, the Revised Standard Version of the Bible, copyright © 1946, 1952, 1971 by the Division of Christian Education of the National Council of the Churches of Christ in the U.S.A. Used by permission.

Scripture quotations marked NLT are taken from the Holy Bible, New Living Translation, copyright © 1996, 2004. Used by permission of Tyndale House Publishers, Inc., Wheaton, Illinois 60189. All rights reserved.

Scriptures quoted from NKJV are from The New King James Version, copyright © 1979, 1980, 1982, Thomas Nelson, Inc., Publishers.

Scripture quotations marked NIV are from the HOLY BIBLE, NEW INTERNATIONAL VERSION®. Copyright © 1973, 1978, 1984 by International Bible Society. Used by permission of Zondervan Publishing House. All rights reserved.

ISBN 13: 978-0-8163-2348-7
ISBN 10: 0-8163-2348-8

09 10 11 12 13 • 5 4 3 2 1

Dedication

To the men and women of law enforcement,
who put their lives on the line every night as we sleep.
Their ministry from God provides safety and security
for our loved ones, our homes, and our communities.

CONTENTS

Chapter One

"THAT'S GRACE"

Out of breath and dripping with rain, I leaned on a back alley dumpster as the man I had just met in a bar aimed a heroin needle at his bulging vein. Just then, a police SUV rolled around the corner and splashed to a stop. Wincing as the window rolled down, I braced for the interrogation. As a pastor and law enforcement chaplain, I had some radical explaining to do.

What, indeed, in name of God, was I doing?

My bizarre adventure began at the Greyhound bus station in Vancouver, British Columbia. I was standing in line to buy a ticket from Canada back to the States, so I could pick up my wife and cats and bring them north to live with me during two years of doctoral studies.

My shoulder sore from lugging my laptop, I set the carrying case at my feet where I could keep an eye on it. The line inched forward. Engrossed in a biography about the missionary William Carey, I shuffled ahead without moving the computer with me.

What happened next is every road warrior's nightmare. When the line moved forward again and I turned to reach for my computer, it was gone! And with it the backup diskette containing a month's worth of summer studies—including three finished papers. Not to mention my passport, student visa, and a hundred dollars' worth of textbooks.

A tsunami of panic swept over me.

"Lord!" I cried, lifting my hands to heaven. Nobody around

acknowledged seeing the thief vanish out the door. After racing outside to scan the perimeter, I summoned station security.

"Where would someone take my computer?" I inquired desperately.

They pointed north to Hastings Street, six blocks away—a seedy assortment of hotel bars and pawn shops that serve as liquidation headquarters for hot property.

As I turned away to chase down my computer, the security chief warned, "Hastings Street is dangerous. Watch who you talk to. Don't even look anybody in the eye as you pass."

With that discomfiting admonition, I ran up the rain-soaked sidewalk, calling on God to help me catch the guy.

I almost did. I stormed through the Savoy Hotel bar just after he had been there trying to hock my machine. They had thrown him out. Which way did he go? They had no idea. At least I got a description: dark hair, medium-tall, skinny, green army-type coat.

Now I could visualize my enemy. With fantasies of street justice pounding with each heartbeat, I hurried ahead, hot on his trail. I hoped for a surprise confrontation: "Stop! Give me my computer!"

If he ran, I would catch up, tackle him, and, if necessary, smash his face. While he regained equilibrium, I would grab my precious laptop and disappear.

I charged from bar to pawn shop, tracking the thief. But his trail had vanished. Word must have gotten out that somebody very big and very angry was after him and that he had better take a siesta somewhere.

Meanwhile, as I intensified my hunt, God's Spirit was working to soothe my spirit. Kinder, gentler thoughts diminished my desperate rage. *So this thief is an old guy my age, and where's his life going? Into the gutter. Hitting the face of that frail man could have knocked him into the concrete curb and caused a brain hemorrhage.*

I might have killed the guy! Imagine a death without Christ after a hopeless life on Hastings Street.

This thought terrified me. The thief's life was a lot more important than my stolen machine. And what was I thinking, anyway? I had never punched anyone in the face in my life!

Thank God I didn't get to hurt that poor thief's hopeless face. As my emotions began to settle, I began noticing the other faces around me, male and female—all hopeless, many scarred and bruised. Evidently, a lot of face-smashing happens on Hastings Street, whether through fights or drunken falls.

What would Jesus do about it? No doubt, He would intercede on behalf of all these broken children of God. By the time I climbed the steps of the police station to report my loss, I found myself repeating a modified version of that eternally incredible prayer from the smashed face of our crucified Savior: *Father forgive him, for he didn't know what he did. Help this poor guy to know Your grace.*

But I still needed my computer!

In a bar, I found a young guy who seemed streetwise and willing to help. I shoved a damp twenty-dollar bill into his grasping hand. "Let's go! You know where these guys hide."

As my drug-addicted deputy led me up the graffiti-filled and condom-strewn alleys behind Hastings Street, he remarked, "Man, I sure hope we catch this guy. We can get him in a corner and really hurt the b@$*&%#!"

By then, my spirit had been sufficiently chastened, so I responded, "But wouldn't it be even better if we gave him grace instead of pain? Yes, I need my computer back, but let's remember that this guy's soul is more important than my machine. So why don't we just get the thing and let him go. Give him grace."

"Grace! What's grace?" my deputy muttered as he ducked into a doorway in that back alley. "Look, man," he said as he pulled a needle from his pocket, "I hate to do this now, but I really need a fix. Hope you don't mind that I shoot up."

"This is your world," I told him.

And so my deputy vigilante bared his arm and aimed the needle at a vein as I stood beside him, watching in helpless horror. Just then, that police SUV roared up, and the officers saw what was happening. There was no place to hide—and here I was a badge-carrying police chaplain from out of the country. In justice they might have loaded us off to jail, or at least taken me in for questioning. Instead, they just smiled and said, "C'mon, fellas, move along."

As we watched them drive off down the alley, I remarked to my friend, "You just asked me what grace is. Well, that's grace."

Our Savior is in the business of letting sinners off the hook—even self-righteous sinners like theology students chasing down computer thieves. If the Almighty did business with us based on justice, we all would die as the due reward of our deeds. We need a refuge, a place of grace to which we can escape.

Escaping to the sanctuary

Long ago the shepherd David, hunted for his life, lamented in total desperation, " 'O that I had wings like a dove! / I would fly away and be at rest' " (Psalm 55:6). Centuries later, Jesus addressed that heart cry: " 'Come to me, all who labor and are heavy laden, and I will give you rest' " (Matthew 11:28).

But that was two thousand years ago. What about us today?

Christianity has much to say about the historic Jesus on the streets of long-ago Galilee, and there is much anticipation of the future eternity with Him. But what about today? What does He offer us today?

The Bible provides a much-overlooked solution. Between the first-century Savior and the future Eternal Lord, Jesus is a very present help in time of trouble: "Since then we have a great high priest who has passed through the heavens, Jesus, the Son of God, let us hold fast our confession" (Hebrews 4:14).

After Christ's resurrection, He went back to heaven to serve in our behalf before God's throne in the sanctuary. "Let us then with confidence draw near to the throne of grace, that we may receive mercy and find grace to help in time of need" (verse 16).

This throne of grace was known in the ancient Jewish sanctuary as the "mercy seat." It was the center of the sanctuary—the place where God dwelt with His people. Through Jesus, we may "with confidence draw near" to God's presence. By contrast, beautiful Queen Esther ventured fearfully into the king's throne room, not knowing whether he would welcome her visit or put her to death. " 'If I perish, I perish,' " she declared (Esther 4:16). But unlike Esther, we don't have to be brave. When we enter God's presence in the sanctuary, we enter a place of refuge, not of threat.

Back during the terrible days of slavery in the United States, the North provided a sanctuary for slaves via the Underground Railroad—an escape trail with safe houses that stretched all the way into Canada. There the slaves found sanctuary.

Civilized society has outlawed that type of slavery, but millions in this land of the free are enslaved just the same. They suffer bondage to dysfunctional relationships, crippling disabilities, indebtedness, miserable jobs, or unemployment. Many who have managed to escape these problems are bound by addiction to others: alcohol, narcotics, materialism, racism, chauvinism, eating disorders, pornography, or gossip. Many more are enslaved to emotional distress, such as guilt, shame, and fear.

From all of that—and so much more—we need a sanctuary. Life is tough, and we crave a place to hide. Sometimes we even desire a lifelong break from the people closest to us. I live in Lincoln, capital of Nebraska. What happens here seldom makes national news. But it did recently when state legislators voted to allow parents to drop off their kids under the age of eighteen at a hospital and give them up forever—no questions asked.

Three dozen parents, mostly of teenagers, drove here from as far away as California to take advantage of our new "safe haven." People everywhere were shocked that parents would do such a thing. Actually, they've been doing it all along—with their spouses! They've been driving to the courthouse and, as it were, dropping off their formerly dearest and best. And in the process, surrendering custody of their kids, at least partially.

How sad when we need a sanctuary from our closest loved ones.

Confidence in the sanctuary

It's even sadder when people need refuge from the God they grew up with. Many forfeit the faith of their youth. They are actually giving up God—the object of faith. It often seems that God isn't doing His job, living up to His promises.

"Ask and it shall be given." *Really?*

It's one thing when we don't get what feels good. But what about when God doesn't give us what seems good? Worse, what if God Himself doesn't seem good but vindictive and arbitrary?

While many people are running away from church, other people hide from God within the church. There is no jungle in which to hide from God that's thicker or more tangled than organized religion, as we generally see it. People hide in ceremonies, arguments, doctrines—even Bible truth that we quarantine in our heads to protect our hearts from God.

And why not, especially if He tortures decent people for eternity? Charles Darwin, father of modern evolutionism, was driven to atheism by the delusion of such a God. Countless others have been as well.

In my case, my childhood religious instruction didn't torment me with fear of an eternally burning hell. I was taught, however, that a relatively brief hell awaited everyone who failed to achieve sinless perfection when heaven's sanctuary closed down and no more mercy was left for struggling sinners. And so I lived many years afraid that God would consign me to hell for being nothing better than a decent person who may have wanted to be like Jesus but fell short.

This book, *God Was There,* records my understanding of the truth about grace that has not only saved my soul but brings me great joy through the sanctuary doctrine. A teaching that once terrorized me now brings me hope, delight, and wonder.

Others of my generation may have, or wish to have, a similar experience. You may be among them. Or you may belong to a younger generation who learned of a kinder, gentler gospel—but not much if anything about heaven's sanctuary.

But somebody is saying, "I don't need Jesus in heaven's sanctuary. I just want Him in my heart."

Actually, the sanctuary is all about Jesus and how He connects and interacts with our hearts and minds. It provides a foundation for organized religion that we can trust. It makes sense of praying in the name of Jesus. It makes us crave God's presence because of His throne of grace.

My goal in these pages is to show how God blesses His people from the sanctuary. From it we receive benefits, including but not limited to

- Grace
- Opportunity for confession
- Opportunity for worship
- God's companionship
- Fellowship with other believers
- Purpose in life
- Spiritual gifting for ministry
- Comfort for our fears
- Correction for our errors
- Healing of spirit, emotions, and bodies
- Education about God, life, and ourselves
- Angelic protection
- Victory over the devil
- Vindication in the judgment
- Insight into the history of good and evil
- Insight into the resolution of evil
- Insight into the future of this world
- Shalom (peace and well-being) here and now
- Social justice for the world
- Solution for pollution and climate change

If I can say this reverently, God's sanctuary exceeds the upscale quality and dignity of New York's exclusive Fifth Avenue shops, the round-the-clock variety of your local Wal-Mart Supercenter, and the inclusive acceptance and unlimited consumption offered without charge at a skid-row soup kitchen. The sanctuary is the one-stop shopping center for whatever we'll need in this life and for eternity.

Speaking of the future . . . in case you fear for your destiny, take comfort from this scripture: "Only in this way [through death] could he set free all who have lived their lives as slaves to the fear of dying" (Hebrews 2:15, NLT). He does this in His role as "our merciful and faithful High Priest" in heaven's sanctuary (verse 17, NLT).

Amazing access to God's presence

Come with me to the Oval Office, the most powerful place in the world. The year is 1962. Gray-suited men solemnly circulate around the room. There are polite knocks at the door, and more enter.

They've earned their right to be here through decades of distinguished civil service. They revel in their right to respectfully address the president as "Mr. President" or as "Sir."

Suddenly, the door to the Oval Office bursts open and a happy little boy toddles in. "Daddy, Daddy!" Nobody seems shocked or offended. President John F. Kennedy grins delightedly as his son jumps onto his lap. The business of the world pauses as father and son exchange kisses and embraces. Then John-John jumps on the carpet and crawls under the desk to play. The business of the world resumes.

The message of the sanctuary is that all of us enjoy John-John access to God through Jesus our High Priest.

It wasn't always so. In Old Testament times, one man had access to the inner sanctuary, the Most Holy Place—earth's Oval Office, if you please. He was the high priest, and he had that access just once a year on the Day of Atonement. He came in trembling, lest his own sin cause him to be struck dead.

It's so different for us. "We who have fled to him for refuge can have great confidence as we hold to the hope that lies before us. This hope is a strong and trustworthy anchor for our souls. It leads us through the curtain into God's inner sanctuary" (Hebrews 6:18, 19, NLT).

We flee—not as Queen Esther, hoping for the golden scepter. The golden scepter was extended to our Representative upon His resurrection. Now, through Him, God's scepter is extended to us. We flee like John-John, confident and affectionate.

We flee—not from God but from the ravages of a troubled and troublesome world. We could not go to God ourselves, and so He came to us in Christ. So now we flee—not in fear but in anticipation of mercy and help at heaven's throne of grace.

I hope in this book to show the benefits that are ours in God's heavenly sanctuary through what Jesus is doing there for us. Each chaplaincy experience that I share will illustrate another aspect of sanctuary teaching. Names have been changed, of course. Beyond this, the stories are true accounts of what I experienced as a law enforcement chaplain in western North America between 1999 and 2005.

Hastings Street becomes a sanctuary

Speaking of which, you may be wondering whether I ever found my stolen computer. I never got it back. But insurance completely covered my loss, and I was able to rewrite the papers.

But something better happened: I saw Hastings Street transformed into a sanctuary. God's Spirit lured me back and transformed my place of pain into an opportunity for ministry. I carried not a computer case but a shopping bag of granola bars and a bunch of long-stem red carnations. I proceeded to greet the confused and smashed faces of my new partners in grace.

Women got not only granola but a flower. It's amazing how a simple carnation can humanize the hardened face of a toothless, flea-bitten prostitute who may never have been given a flower in her entire wretched lifetime. Several wanted me to pray that they could escape from their life of sin and find grace in heaven's sanctuary.

It felt wonderful to walk up and down Hastings Street as if I owned the place, mingling with the addicts and prostitutes. When I saw a guy connecting with one of the women, I interrupted, "Hey, man, do you know whose daughter she is? She's a child of *God*!"

"She is?" the guy said, stepping back from her. "What about me?" And so there was another fine conversation as he abandoned the woman to encounter her Lord.

I became one of the addicts on Hastings Street—hooked on the thrill of ministry there.

People kept asking, "Who are you with? Where are you from?" I told them, "I'm from Jesus. I lost a computer here four days ago—but I'm not here because of that. I'm here because of lost people! Your soul is a lot more precious than a machine."

Later, as I contentedly leaned against a wall surveying the late afternoon scene, someone approached wearing a backpack stashed no doubt with all manner of unmentionables. "What do you need?" he whispered. I smiled and said, "I need the Lord, man! How about you?"

Another time, a young guy wearing a Cleveland Indians baseball cap asked if I had a Bible, which I pulled out of my own stashed backpack.

When finally my feet got tired and my throat dry, I strolled into a now familiar pool hall and ordered some orange juice. Another refreshing experience, sitting there amid swirling cigarette smoke while relishing all the mission opportunities. No wonder Jesus spent so much of His ministry hanging out with such people.

To summarize the saga of Hastings Street, out of my pain I received more joy than I could ever find on the white sands of Hawaii. How gratifying to see hunchbacked women still cradling their carnations hours after receiving them. Every woman needs a flower—especially women with smashed faces. It's all about grace—God's throne of grace in heaven's sanctuary.

Nothing honors and cheers God more than seeing faces smashed by sin smiling as His sons and daughters and lifting trembling hands high for His celestial fix from the sanctuary.

Questions for Reflection and Discussion

1. Which of the many benefits of the sanctuary mean the most to you?
2. How would you describe God's grace? (Describe it—don't define it.)
3. When did you first understand God's grace? Or have you never really grasped it?
4. What is your greatest barrier to experiencing God's grace?
5. What trauma have you experienced that makes you need a sanctuary?

Chapter Two

TRUE CONFESSION

"Father, I have sinned! I killed her! I don't know how, I don't know why! I was drunk, I guess."

The tousled blond twenty-three-year-old had just been arrested, but Brad requested a police chaplain instead of a lawyer. So here I was, watching him rock back and forth like a suppliant at Jerusalem's Wailing Wall. I noticed dried blood on his fingernails.

Being a Protestant, I never had anyone address me spiritually as "father." And nobody had ever confessed sins to me—much less first-degree murder. The detectives said that it had been a particularly brutal killing.

I had spent much of the previous night comforting Brad's mother, the head nurse in a hospital emergency room. She became hysterical when police visited her, seeking clues about his whereabouts. She couldn't believe her "gentle boy" deserved suspicion of such a crime.

"I know Brad didn't do it!" she sobbed. "I didn't raise him to be a murderer!"

As a boy, Brad was so tenderhearted that he brought home a sick baby bird and nurtured it to health. But during his teens, they moved to Las Vegas, and he fell in with a rough crowd. He got hooked on drugs and drinking.

Her words denied what I sensed her heart realized: Brad had become capable of radical violence. I did my best to console her. "Whatever choices Brad might be making with his life, it doesn't change the fact that you've obviously been a caring, sacrificial mother. I'm with the police department and I can assure you that Brad will be in good hands after he is arrested."

My words seemed to give her a little comfort, so I went home.

At daybreak, police caught Brad and called me back. As the sergeant led me to the holding room, I confirmed to Brad that whatever I heard would be confidential, due to clergy-client privilege. Then, as soon as the door was shut, Brad's confession of murder gushed out like vomit.

What should I do? Urge him to confess to the detectives? Open my Bible and explain how sinners can be saved? I decided to listen some more before talking.

After Brad got the awful story off his chest, he seemed relieved. They say confession is good for the soul, although it didn't do any good for his victim, now in the county morgue.

As I was wondering what to say, Brad jolted me into action by asking, "What shall I do now?" There was only one answer to that question: " 'Believe on the Lord Jesus Christ, and you will be saved' " (Acts 16:31, NKJV).

Somehow I couldn't share that verse as easily as I always had before, even when talking to *convicted* murderers. It's one thing in a prison ministry sermon to say, "No matter what you've done, God is ready right here and right now to forgive you." But with a murderer fresh from the crime scene with blood still on his hands, forgiveness didn't quite seem appropriate. Besides, Brad hadn't turned himself in—they caught him at a friend's apartment. So what was this confessional about? Saying magic words to receive a sacrament of remission?

I didn't want any part of such a charade. Brad mentioned being drunk when he killed the victim, as if that partially excused his crime. And if he was in denial of his guilt, where was the contrition that goes with genuine confession?

Confession means agreeing with God

You see, in Scripture, the basic meaning of confession is to agree with God. And since God says sin is wrong, confession doesn't try to diminish one's guilt. Rather, confession implies repentance—aligning ourselves with God's hatred of sin so that we agree with His condemnation of it and then turn away from it.

Brad had committed first-degree murder, but I wasn't hearing what seemed to be a first-degree confession. And given the lingering effects of liquor, I didn't think he was even capable of repentance yet. Only God knows the heart, though.

Brad had asked me a question, and it was my job to provide an answer. So I explained that he had two problems with guilt—first, with the law of the land, and then with the law of God. I couldn't help him deal with the charges that he might face from the district attorney. Only a lawyer could advise him regarding those. I also told him right up front that he shouldn't expect me to testify on his behalf. I did not want any involvement with the legal process, one way or the other.

I told Brad my business with him was to help him deal with his guilt before God. "This doesn't mean saying magic words of confession to a priest," I said. "Confessing means that we agree with God's judgment that those who break His Ten Commandments are worthy of death—and you tell me you just murdered somebody.

"That's where Jesus enters the picture. Long ago, Jesus came to this earth and became a human being. He lived a perfect life on our behalf and then died on the cross. He died for our sins while praying that His murderers would be forgiven. And He is just as eager for you to be forgiven!

"Brad, do you see God's good news here? Because of Jesus, now you don't have to die an eternal death if you are willing to confess Him as your Savior."

I read him Romans 10:9, "If you confess with your mouth that Jesus is Lord and believe in your heart that God raised him from the dead, you will be saved" (NLT). Then I continued, "You might die in an electric chair or live the rest of your life behind bars. I'm not going to ask God to save you from that. But you can choose right now to be saved for eternal life in heaven."

Next I turned to Proverbs 28:13, "He who conceals his transgressions will not prosper, / but he who confesses and forsakes them will obtain mercy."

"So, Brad," I said, "if you confess agreement with God's judgment that you are a sinner worthy of death and confess your belief that Jesus died that death for you, then your sin is forgiven—not because the words of confession are some kind of magic but because of God's gift of Jesus and your agreement with it."

I realized that I was telling Brad too much for him to fully understand, especially in his condition. But maybe some of it got through.

"Do you understand any of this, Brad?" I asked, looking at him closely. He nodded thoughtfully and willingly.

"Would you like to pray with me about this?"

"Yes."

So we did. And that was it. I stood up to leave.

"One more thing, Brad. What we just read in the Bible about confessing your sins and not hiding them could be quite a bit different from the advice you might get from an attorney. I don't know. Just remember that it's your decision about whether to confess to any charges you face. Do what you know to be right, no matter what the legal consequences may be. You might spend the rest of your life behind bars, but your spirit can be free in Jesus."

Brad nodded and thanked me. He asked me if I would visit his young daughter, and I assured him that I would if his mother would arrange it. As I turned to leave, Brad looked relieved—even, perhaps, peaceful.

My false guilt

Maybe Brad had peace now, but I didn't. Not after walking past the room where detectives were struggling to piece his case together. I knew everything but could tell them nothing.* This left me feeling like I was party to an ugly secret. Darlene, my wife, noticed I wasn't feeling well

---

* This experience didn't happen in California, where I was forbidden to visit prisoners by the county in which I served. A prison chaplain cared for those incarcerated. My job was only to support the officers and their families of the ten local, county, state, and federal law enforcement agencies that we served, assisting them with their professional emergencies and personal spiritual needs. This actually was a good policy because it saved me from conflict-of-interest situations like this one with Brad, which occurred in another western state.

when I got home. She thought that it was because I had been up half the night with Brad's mom.

"No, it's not that," I told her, "but I can't tell you what it is."

I couldn't talk to anyone about Brad's confession. Two things about it worried me. First, the conspiracy of silence I shared with a murderer, which made me feel even more terrible after seeing the victim's grieving family. They were desperate for information that I could not tell them. Meanwhile, Brad decided upon his lawyer's advice to plead innocent to the charge of first-degree murder. So much for true confession!

The other thing that troubled me deeply was the whole idea of grace. Something about grace being applied in Brad's situation just didn't seem right. I often taught that grace was radical forgiveness, but this seemed a bit too radical. Brad had just murdered a helpless woman while assaulting her brutally. She was dead and gone, and her family would never forget their grief. Was it really appropriate for Brad to just come away clean, instantly forgiven, as if he hadn't done anything wrong?

It's one thing to teach grace intellectually as a fundamental Bible doctrine; it's another thing to deal with grace emotionally when God seems too merciful for our sense of justice. You can assure a drug addict who gets caught spraying graffiti that God's grace is all for him. Amen! But Brad was a heavy-duty sinner.

I had to keep reminding myself that Jesus prayed for murderers to be forgiven. Besides, as a member of the fallen human race redeemed at the Cross, Brad had already received God's wrath in the person of Jesus, his Savior. Such is the gospel, and if I didn't embrace such grace, I couldn't be a Christian.

Indeed, the gospel is all about grace, A–Z. There is no holding back the floodgates of mercy, so I had better get used to it. Besides, grace is the only way for my own sorry soul to be saved.

A rather morbid but helpful illustration came to mind: At the county morgue, the body of the woman Brad had murdered would look far worse than that of a man who died that night of a drug overdose. But both corpses would be equally lifeless. Even so, every human being outside of Christ is "dead in trespasses and sins" (Ephesians 2:1, NKJV).

Some have messed up more flagrantly than others, but, were it not for grace, my soul would be just as hopeless as Brad's. Without Jesus, divine forgiveness would be inappropriate for either of us.

So what difference is there between Brad and me—or you—in heaven's judgment? "There is no distinction; since all have sinned and fall short of the glory of God, they are justified by his grace as a gift, through the redemption which is in Christ Jesus" (Romans 3:22–24).

"Just can't forgive myself"

It was conviction of my own need for grace that finally allowed me to feel peace about Brad's forgiveness. But grace is so wonderful it can be hard to take personally. Frequently, people lament, "Maybe God has forgiven me, but I just can't forgive myself." Sometimes we hear this from someone who, like Brad, has sinned notoriously. Other times it's somebody who doesn't even seem to be a sinner. Either way, grace is difficult to grasp for a tender conscience struggling to forgive itself.

But let's remember our Friend in heaven's sanctuary, interceding for us: "Who is to condemn? It is Christ Jesus, who died, yes, who was raised from the dead, who is at the right hand of God, who indeed intercedes for us?" (Romans 8:34).

We are not judges of all the earth, *so we don't have the right either to forgive ourselves or to condemn ourselves.* That's God's job. And He accepts, not rejects, all those who come to Him through Jesus: "Who dares accuse us whom God has chosen for his own? No one—for God himself has given us right standing with himself" (verse 33, NLT).

So Father and Son work together for us in heaven's sanctuary.

"There is therefore now no condemnation for those who are in Christ Jesus" (verse 1). No condemnation in Christ! To believe otherwise is inappropriate. We all know it's wrong to condemn other people. But did you know *it's just as wrong to condemn yourself,* when heaven's Judge has forgiven you?

As a teenager, I certainly felt like condemning myself when a speaker at a youth rally gave a talk titled "Slightly Soiled, Greatly Reduced in Value." His point was that just as department store clothing is less valuable when it gets soiled—even just a bit—so with teenagers. We had better behave ourselves, or we lose value with God.

Nothing could be further from the truth. Our sinfulness does not make us less valuable to God. How do we know? Because "while we were still sinners, Christ died for us" (Romans 5:8, NKJV).

A personal experience helped me understand that. I used to wear contact lenses and had to be careful. Those nearly invisible slivers of plastic could be hard to find if dropped.

One night, I was tired and careless as I was taking them out and one bounced off the sink and—oh no!—into the cat litter box. So what did I do? Condemn it as filthy and go buy another one? No. Tired as I was, I searched through that loaded litter box (I hadn't emptied it that day) until I found my little lost treasure.

Was it dirty? More than I can tell you in print. Yet it was just as precious as the one still in my eye. Lost, filthy, but every bit as valuable. That's why I went through so much trouble to save it.

Lovability is not a human quality

Something else about our sins—they don't make us less lovable. Did you know this? *Lovability is a quality in God's eyes, not a quality of human character or personality.* We may infer this from both John 3:16 and 1 John 3:16: "God so loved the world that he gave his only Son." "By this we know love, that he laid down his life for us."

The world teaches something quite different about lovability. You are lovable if you are cute, smart, rich, slim, powerful, or popular. Hollywood has even quantified this. Do you know what your "Q Score" is?[1]

"The Q Score is a way to measure the familiarity and appeal of a brand, company, celebrity, cartoon character or television show. The higher the Q Score, the more well-known and well thought of the item or person being scored is."[2] Their actual numbers are a closely guarded trade secret.

There's TV Q, Sports Q, and believe it or not, even Dead Q! " 'Dead Q' measures the current familiarity and appeal of deceased personalities in a variety of categories to determine current targeted audience attraction."[3]

I have a neighbor across the street seven houses down who was a finalist in the *America's Got Talent* TV program. I hear he does a pretty good Elvis. Given the number and success of Elvis's impersonators, it's fair to guess that he enjoys a really high "Dead Q" rating. The next time I see my neighbor, I'll ask if he knows where Elvis ranks among the 150 dead legends tracked by Q. Maybe he's even number one. I'll bet if he knew he was still so lovable, he'd want to roll over in his grave. Obviously, the world's concept of lovability doesn't do much for the people it celebrates.

I'm glad things are different with God, who doesn't worship dead memories but lavishes His love upon everyone alive, cute or otherwise. Let's take our cue from God. Remember, there's nothing we can do to make ourselves more lovable than we already are because lovability isn't a quality of human character but a quality of God's character of love.

This gets very personal with God. Not only does He love the mass of this world's unlovely humanity, but He loves little old me and you. How do I know? On the cross, Jesus "loved me and gave himself for me" (Galatians 2:20, NIV).

God has a big stake in us. Think of what He has invested—the life of His precious Son! From that sacrifice, we receive eternal life. But what does God get? He gets us!

The apostle Paul prayed that God's people would understand "the riches of *his* glorious inheritance in the saints" (Ephesians 1:18; emphasis added). Salvation is more than God feeling sorry for sinners as you might feel pity for a scraggly kitten in the snow. No, God delights in us for His own sake. We really are that special to Him.

Just today my wife and I got a Christmas card from a local dentist who played as a linebacker on the 1997 National Championship college football team, the Nebraska Huskers. Darlene babysat his baby until the child graduated into toddler care.

Travis and his wife simply delight in their little girl. Every Tuesday afternoon, he closes down his dental office and takes little Emmy on a field trip—just the two of them. Baby Emmy couldn't walk, so he carried her on their adventures. When she dirtied her diaper, he didn't scold her.

He just got her cleaned up, and they moved on. This little baby with her soiled diapers was immeasurably more valuable to him than his National Championship ring.

Emmy has no idea who her dad was or anything about a Q Score. Nor does she have any idea how incredibly precious she is.

But she's learning.

We can be learning too, and heaven's sanctuary can help us understand.

Even murderers

And Brad? What happened to him? He eventually pled guilty (or I wouldn't be able to tell you his story, even anonymously). This turned out well for his legal situation. Just a swab from his fingernails for a DNA test might have been enough to convict him. Brad may have spared himself the electric chair by coming clean on the record before all the evidence was in.

Before his court date, he asked me for printed Bible studies. I provided them, wondering whether he might want them just to impress a jury with how religious he had become. But after he was sentenced and taken away to serve his life in prison, he still wanted me to mail books and studies. He also connected with the prison chaplain and fellow Christian prisoners of hope.

Evidently, Brad's repentance was sincere, after all. The morning after he took somebody else's life, he received the gift of eternal life for himself.

It's all about grace—for him and for us.

Questions for Reflection and Discussion

1. Why do many parents feel responsible for an adult child's behavior?
2. Since confession is "agreeing with God," what are some of its positive aspects?

3. What benefits does God Himself receive from saving us?
4. How are some ways you are tempted to exploit God's grace?
5. Why does God consider you lovable?

Chapter Three

FALSE GUILT

I've never had a gun pointed at my head. But one day, I was summoned to help three people who suffered that trauma and who then felt guilty about surviving it.

Ringing the California side of Lake Tahoe are several charming tourist towns. One of them has a friendly little bank with a rustic, wood-paneled lobby. One morning, the peace of that place was shattered by an armed robber, who stole more than cash. He took peace of mind from three fine employees. It was my task to help them regain a sense of normalcy.

Dispatch sent me a day later to do a defusing, which involves helping the victims process the emotions and perceptions they were dealing with. Ideally, I would also have debriefed them immediately after the trauma to help shape their initial impressions before the shock wore off. But now they had some time to think about what happened and form initial conclusions, which weren't necessarily accurate or helpful to their recovery.

The bank manager agreed to let me conduct the defusing in the privacy of her office so the victims could talk openly. Soon the three of them—two tellers and one assistant manager—were reflecting on their experience. They said the robber had shoved a gun in their faces, demanded cash, grabbed the bags of money, and roared off. Police caught him before he could get to I-80 and escape the state.

Only those who have stared into the barrel of a loaded gun brandished by a crazed criminal know what those tellers and their manager were feeling. First of all, terrified apprehension—when would the next robbery happen? They also suffered guilt. The women were feeling bad about the man getting away with money that people had entrusted to them and for which they were accountable. The assistant manager was feeling especially guilty. Why? Because as a supervisor, it was his responsibility to provide a safe working environment, and he felt that he had failed his employees. They also were his friends. Plus, he had a male's natural instinct to defend females, and after the robbery, he wasn't feeling like much of a man. So he was down on himself both as a male and as a manager.

I asked the women if they had any response to what he was saying. They emphatically assured him that he hadn't failed them at all, adding, "Your calm strength kept us from freaking out!" I added my affirmation that he did the right thing by not trying to play Superman, which would have endangered them all.

In fact, all three employees did exactly what they were supposed to do—they got the armed robber out of the building and into the great outdoors where nobody was trapped in close quarters. The police swooped in on a safe stretch of highway and took him down. They even recovered all the cash.

So I congratulated them all as having done exactly what both common sense and bank policy stipulated. "You guys are heroes!"

They smiled for the first time that morning. As I shook their hands, their faces showed obvious relief. We joined hands and prayed, after which they even joked a bit about what happened. Fear and false guilt were gone.

Appropriate versus inappropriate guilt

Those bank tellers had felt guilty, even though they had broken no laws. By contrast, most criminals claim innocence. Plan A would be to deny having committed the crime. Because this bank robber was caught with the looted money, he probably would resort to Plan B. That would be excusing his behavior, posturing as either a victim or a hero who desperately needed money for a worthy cause. "My girlfriend's baby had to have milk!"

Some conscientious people who would never wish to break a rule live under a perpetual cloud of guiltiness. Meanwhile, many career criminals seem incapable of guilt or shame. When arrested, they are belligerent, profane, and abusive to the officers—and quite self-righteous throughout the ride to jail.

God's sanctuary has a plan of resolving both problems. Before we discuss that resolution, can we make this personal? That is, where do you stand? Are you more likely to deny guilt or to go overboard in feeling bad about your failures?

I confess that my predisposition is to succumb to inappropriate guilt, most likely because of my upbringing, specifically from my father, now deceased. And he would be proud of me telling you this. He purposely raised us to be afraid of him and afraid of God. I have his Bible, in which—believe it or not—he actually crossed out the word *grace* and wrote in *fear*.

My father learned to appreciate fear when he was drafted into the army during World War II and rushed off to Europe. Basic training instilled fear into the draftees because within weeks, they would be thrown into action against highly trained Nazi forces. Their survival and success depended upon the discipline instilled upon them through tactics of force and fear. And he learned his lessons well.

On March of 1945, his division of the Seventh U.S. Army crossed the Siegfried Line into Germany. Just past the Saar River, he discovered a minefield and alerted his battalion. For the next four hours, he single-handedly defused that minefield, an act for which he earned the nation's third-highest medal of valor, the Silver Star. His army burst on through Nazi Germany to help liberate the prisoners in the Dachau concentration camp.

Upon marrying a German woman and returning to the United States, he decided to raise his family the way he was trained in the army. He delighted in making us fear him and fear God. I remember waking up every morning at 5:45 as he came down the steps toward my room, angry, like a drill sergeant. I started having panic attacks every time I was alone with him.

Seven times my mother ran away from him with us three boys, but we always ran out of money and had to come back home. Finally, we got away for good—but it was too late for me to escape a lifetime proclivity to fear. That emotion was so tattooed on my personality and character that more than half a century later, my fundamental emotional reaction to life is still fear. I am fundamentally a fearful, broken person—except when I look up to the sanctuary and see our loving God.*

I wanted you to have that background so you can see why I'm so excited about the sanctuary. In a passage of Scripture that culminates with the news of Christ's intercession for us, we find this marvelous assurance: "You did not receive the spirit of slavery to fall back into fear, but you have received the spirit of sonship. When we cry 'Abba! Father!' it is the Spirit himself bearing witness with our spirit that we are children of God, and if children, then heirs, heirs of God and fellow heirs with Christ" (Romans 8:15–17).

I need this type of nurturing every day from God's Word.

People who shun accountability

The same Lord who comforts the afflicted also knows when He has to afflict the comfortable. Some people actually might need their guardian angel to kick them in the pants now and then! As a police chaplain, I've met a lot of them—abusive and arrogant yet somehow self-righteous about it.

I think of a man grazed by a car as he was crossing the road, drunk. He was fetching beer from a convenience store, accompanied by his Boston terrier. The road was dark, and the driver who hit him as he wandered across hadn't even seen him.

When paramedics arrived, the dog, which had also been injured, was still at the side of his unworthy master. When they took him off to the hospital, the little dog limped through the woods to the trailer where they lived. The man's eighty-year-old mother let the dog in.

---

* I wrote a book about my experience, *My Tortured Conscience*. It's long out of print, but available at no cost on my Web site, *www.securingyourfuture.org.*

I arrived shortly after, and the precious little terrier greeted me lovingly, even with blood all over its legs and belly. We did what we could for the dog, and then I took the mother to the hospital to visit her son. Although basically uninjured and able to think clearly, he seemed to have no sense of the havoc that his latest episode of drinking had caused his dear old mother and his faithful little dog.

I recognize that there is a medical component to alcoholism and that therefore, it is properly called a disease. But there also is a moral component to maintaining an addiction that involves deception, manipulation, and blatant selfishness. Lying to oneself or to one's loved ones or employer is a choice—a fact often overlooked by those who insist on making excuses for those who refuse help for their addictions.

Guilt is not good for addiction recovery

Perhaps we deny the moral component of addicted people's choices because we know that loading guilt on them only worsens addictive behavior. And secular society has no place to go with guilt—whereas we have the heavenly sanctuary with God's throne of grace.

Grace, not denial, is God's solution to guilt.

The truth is that I'm not OK, and neither are you. Not only are we born in sin, but we also have indulged it gleefully ever since our "terrible twos." What we should do with this guilt is to confess it and then cast it upon our Savior.

Actually, probably all of us are addictive in one way or another. There are the classic addictions of alcohol and narcotics. Eating disorders express addiction, as does illicit or obsessive sexuality—whether with real people or with pornography. Compulsive gambling is now acknowledged as an addiction, as is shoplifting and even out-of-control shopping.

And how about other forms of greed that might cause one to overwork in relation to family responsibilities? It's called *workaholism*. (Other people have couchaholism!) Maybe a mindless drive toward success, or winning for its own sake rather than for a valid purpose, is a powerful addiction for many otherwise respectable people.

What about sportsaholics or hunters who are out of control?

And consider this question: Can someone be addicted to another person? Isn't enabling an alcoholic—actually living the lie of that addict—an addiction in itself? Isn't it wrong to be more committed to making somebody else feel good than to maintain one's own propriety and integrity?

How about gossip? Or subtle bragging, showing off, and other forms of pride? (Full disclosure here: I have to examine everything I write to ensure that I don't indulge an addiction to the approval of others—basically, to get myself noticed.)

Even harmless hobbies can cross a line and become obsessions—addictions. Something may be harmless in itself, or even good, but if it gets out of balance, it becomes an addiction. So, even religion can become an addiction! An addiction to rules as a means to promoting one's own righteousness is legalism—a religion based upon *shoulds* and *oughts* instead of God's grace. (More about this later.)

Anything that throws life out of balance can be an addiction, as can anything that is done compulsively as a substitute for something else that we ought to be doing. There are many complex psychological and physiological factors that contribute to addiction. No wonder the Bible teaches, "The whole head is sick, / and the whole heart is faint" (Isaiah 1:5). The umbrella word for the moral component in all of this is *sin*.

Grace is God's addiction management

So I respectfully suggest that all of us have addictive issues of some kind or another to manage. The solution to guilt is grace. "Let us then with confidence draw near to the throne of grace, that we may receive mercy and find grace to help in time of need" (Hebrews 4:16).

This is the heart of God's sanctuary, where Jesus is eager and willing to intercede for us and stand with us, no matter our addiction. God's sanctuary is heaven's addiction recovery center. It's the place where we flee for refuge. When we are stressed or tempted, instead of escaping into addiction, God invites us to flee to His throne of grace to find mercy and grace.

A sense of God's loving grace cures us from one of the core components to addictive behavior—the sense of victimhood. All of us have been wounded and mistreated in life, some more than others. Many of us have been abused, sexually or otherwise. While the pain of abuse should never be denied or minimized, we shouldn't use our abuse as an excuse for irresponsibility and sink into addictive behavior.

Grace cures us from victimhood, as we'll see later. The Bible says, "Where sin abounded, grace abounded much more" (Romans 5:20, NKJV). God is greater than whatever has happened in our past, and He has promised to work all things for good to those willing to love Him and fulfill His purpose for their lives (Romans 8:28).

Learning how this happens takes lots of spiritual mentoring and a deep knowledge of God's Word, with its promises and admonitions. So you have a learning process. This is the heart of what the Bible calls being a disciple. Jesus invites us to learn from Him (Matthew 11:29). In the same verse, He says, " 'Take my yoke upon you.' " So, to learn from Him, we must commit ourselves to working with Him.

We all need lots of love and healing. Sometimes we'll take two steps forward and one step back—or even three back. But God's grace will keep us going for the long haul. That's why Jesus could say, " 'The one who endures to the end will be saved' " (Matthew 24:13, NLT).

God doesn't ask us to be strong enough to overcome anything. He does require us to be truthful with ourselves, with Him, and with each other.

I heard one person remark, I hope merely as a bad joke, "God and I have a good thing going. He enjoys forgiving, and I enjoy sinning. It's a win-win situation." Actually, God's not in the business of playing games with our souls. He loves us too much to enable our addictions and perpetuate our dysfunctions.

Long ago, Jesus went for a walk on a Sabbath day. He passed a place where there were many people who were suffering. He went up to a seriously miserable man and asked, " 'Do you want to be made well?' " (John 5:6, NKJV).

Not everyone does.

How about you?

Questions for Reflection and Discussion

1. At what point is it appropriate for a dysfunctional family to separate (not divorce)?
2. How does it matter whether we view addiction as a physical disease or a sin?
3. Are you more inclined toward false guilt or to abusing God's grace?
4. What in your upbringing influenced your answer to question number 3?
5. What "respectable" addictions do you struggle with?

Chapter Four

JUSTICE FROM THE SANCTUARY

Of all the tragedies that call out chaplains, nothing is more heartbreaking than suicide. It's sad enough when elderly cancer victims euthanize themselves, although we might understand why they would gulp a handful of sleeping pills with their morning coffee to escape another miserable day on the way to a slow and sure demise. But what could be more wrenching and perplexing than a teenager killing himself after an evening of fun at a football game? *All of life before him—yet he feels that he has nothing to live for?*

The call came Sunday night from a small town off I-80 in the lower Sierras. A high school student fatally shot himself with a rifle. Hours later, they found his body slumped behind the wheel of a pickup truck in the deserted parking lot of a lumberyard. On the dashboard was a cryptic note in his distinctive handwriting that didn't explain much.

Why did Jason murder himself? He was a favorite with fellow students and faculty, good at sports, and great with girls. So why would he end a life of popularity and promise?

That question haunted everyone at school the next morning. Several of us chaplains met with the faculty at 7:00 A.M. to discuss a strategy for comforting the students—and the teachers.

After we worked through the sensitivities related to separation of church and state at a public high school, the principal suggested we set up headquarters in the library. She let students come and go there all day, and teachers invited the chaplains to each classroom so the kids knew who we were.

We served cookies and cocoa in the library and put poster boards and color markers on the tables and encouraged the kids to compose tributes to Jason. Some drew pictures or cartoons of their memories. Others created poetry. Most just penned words of sadness and hung around to talk.

We chaplains circulated through the library unobtrusively, commenting on the posters and conversing with kids who wanted to talk. We mentioned God only if they brought up religion.

They certainly did. The biggest question was, Why did God let it happen?

Why do the innocent suffer?

A true but superficial answer would be that God didn't pull the trigger on Jason's gun. The deeper, unanswered question is, If there is a good and powerful God, why is the world so full of death and dysfunction?

Secular philosophers, from ancient times on, have not been shy about saying, "If there is a God, he is either powerless in the face of prevailing evil, or he is indifferent to that evil, and thus not good enough to want to do anything about it. Either he isn't good or he isn't sovereign. Because evil exists, he cannot be both good and sovereign."

As a chaplain, I can relate to the feeling of being powerless. How often I've wrung my hands in frustration at being unable to find a lost hiker or resuscitate a dead motorcyclist. If I could resolve the situation, I'd do it in a heartbeat. But God, being omnipotent, doesn't have the limitations I have. So why doesn't He do more to help us? You don't have to be an atheist or agnostic to wonder what's going on with God when things go wrong and He doesn't seem to care.

Some would scold us at this point: "Believers aren't supposed to feel that way." The fact is, we often do. Even the most faithful suffer doubts. Faith isn't the absence of doubt but the choice to stay faithful to God despite our doubts.

Ironically, if it weren't for God's glorious promises, we wouldn't have so many doubts. They raise the expectations that life's realities crush. Jesus said God loves His creatures so much that He notices even when a little sparrow falls to the ground. And because we are of much more value than many sparrows, we can take heart that God is watching over us.

Upon hearing Jesus' words, one little girl said, "Well, why does God just watch the sparrows fall? If I were God, I would catch the sparrows and not let them fall to the ground where a cat could eat them."

It's a legitimate question—why do innocent people, and even animals, suffer?

Why don't guilty people suffer?

Another question is why the guilty so often seem to escape punishment or even consequences. I guess all of us can come up with a list of grievances about why people who deserve to go to jail or to be fined manage to escape their punishment. But there's another way to look at it too: how many times do we deserve punishment and manage to escape it?

Police tell us that the average motorist breaks traffic laws eight times whenever he or she gets behind the wheel. God only knows how many times *we* don't get what we deserve.

Let me give you a personal story about just that. I had moved from Washington, D.C., to West Virginia, tasked with leading a group of fellow students to start a church in Point Pleasant, a village along the Ohio River. As summer ended, we had a little group going, but they couldn't afford a pastor, and the local conference had no funds either.

So, my buddy Steve and I decided to stay behind. We lived in the boiler room of a church in Huntington, West Virginia, and sold Christian books in the neighborhood. Every weekend we drove along the river to Point Pleasant so we could care for the church we were raising up. When our old, blue Ford broke down, we hitchhiked.

We had no place to stay in Point Pleasant. No problem! We just broke into an abandoned house, brushed aside the mold and rat droppings, and slept there. At dawn, we slipped out of the house and went to a twenty-four-hour Laundromat. In the back room, we took turns bathing in a bucket, while the other one kept watch. Then we went out and led the church services!

One day, we were speeding along the Ohio side of the river on Highway 7. We came to a village famous for being the site of a speed trap. I think most of its revenue came from its busy traffic court—about the most exciting thing happening in town. Sure enough, I got trapped, ticketed, and summoned to judgment.

I didn't have the money to pay the ticket, so I went before the judge to plead my case. He never let me make my argument. As soon as I told him I was doing Christian work, he said, "Young man, am I hearing you say that you work for the Lord?"

"Yes, Your Honor."

"Well then, the Lord is responsible for your ticket! You won't have to pay it."

I noticed disappointment on the face of the police officer who had ticketed me and was there to accuse me before the court. He certainly wasn't happy, and I can't blame him. It was unfair that I was getting off free.

But the case was closed. The judge pounded his gavel and that was the end of it.

I felt so relieved and happy that I naively said, "Judge, I would like to offer a prayer for you and for this court."

"You mean, right here and now?"

"Yes, sir."

"Well, you go right ahead. Order in the court. Everybody bow your heads."

So I prayed, asking the Lord to bless everybody there, including the judge and the policeman. I also prayed that I wouldn't speed again. "In Jesus' name, Amen."

With that, I triumphantly exited the courtroom. The police officer didn't look any happier than before my prayer. Again, I can't blame him. He was just doing his job, and I had managed to escape justice.

The officer may have had some question about whether I deserved to be cleared of charges. But ultimately, his problem was with the judge.

After all, the judge had vindicated me. He hadn't even let me open my mouth to answer the just charges of the law against me.

The same issue arises when a prisoner wins early parole. People wonder, *Why is this guy running loose? I thought he was supposed to be locked up.* There's a question about the parolee himself, but the real issue is with the parole board. Why did the chairman of the parole board let him go free?

May I suggest this reverently: God is the Chair of heaven's parole board. He sets us free from condemnation. The devil, our accuser, doesn't like it. But his problem is with God—what right does He have to set us free? How is He fair and just in vindicating some, while condemning others?

The sanctuary—audit center of the universe

Long ago, Asaph, a writer of musical poetry who worked with King David, found himself quite upset when he looked around him and saw so many lawbreakers prospering while decent people suffered. He was quite disturbed about this, he said, "until I went into the sanctuary of God; / then I perceived their end" (Psalm 73:17). The sanctuary is where God reveals Himself to His creation.

Sometimes grace and truth have conflicting claims upon leadership. Ethical yet compassionate managers know something of this dilemma between mercy and justice. All organizations need rules governing operation; chaos results when laws aren't upheld. Therefore, violations of company law must be dealt with for the good of everyone.

Suppose you have a store policy that no employee can shoplift merchandise—a good law that must be enforced. But there's a poor sales clerk who keeps shoplifting clothes for her baby. How do you show her mercy without making allowances for others who could argue their own circumstances as an excuse to steal? How do you forgive the lawbreaker without opening the floodgates of lawlessness?

Such is God's problem. Mercy for sinners and justice against sin have conflicting claims upon His loving character. He had to find a way to maintain grace, as the tender heavenly Father, and truth, as the moral Governor of His creation.

God solved His moral dilemma through Christ's sacrifice at Calvary. Jesus was the One "whom God set forth as a propitiation by His blood, through faith, to demonstrate His righteousness, because in His forbearance God had passed over the sins that were previously committed" (Romans 3:25, NKJV).

God has nothing to hide from His creation. Being the Sovereign Almighty, He wouldn't have to answer anyone's questions. But to sustain trust in His government of love, He allows Himself to be audited by the heavenly universe. Thus it becomes evident how He has been faithful amid the unfaithfulness of those who resist His authority and disbelieve His character.

"What if some did not believe? Will their unbelief make the faithfulness of God without effect? Certainly not! Indeed, let God be true but every man a liar. As it is written: / 'That You may be justified in Your words, / And may overcome when You are judged' " (verses 3, 4, NKJV). This divine overcoming in the celestial audit of His government will answer every question.

I'm sure the angels themselves wonder why some humans are vindicated and others condemned when nobody's perfect and even the finest human beings have their faithless moments. Before God takes us up to heaven, He allows the angels to have their own questions answered about us—ultimately about Him. Jesus will confess us as His own before the angels and before His Father (Revelation 3:5; Luke 12:8).

Finally, the entire universe will be able to proclaim, " 'Just and true are Your ways, / O King of the saints!' " (Revelation 15:3, NKJV). During the thousand years after Jesus comes, we humans will have the opportunity to get answers to our questions about God. The final execution of divine punishment that Scripture portrays occurs only after this millennium (Revelation 20).

Kidnap victims restored

There is one particular experience I had as a law enforcement chaplain that illustrates how God will ultimately ensure that the captives of injustice will be set free. On a sunny Sunday afternoon in the autumn, I was doing a ride-along with a veteran sergeant. We cruised around town, watching for speeders and checking back alleys for suspicious loiterers.

The sergeant liked having me along as an extra set of eyes. He was glad for my ears as well—he enjoyed talking. The Oakland Raiders, mortgage interest rates, local politics, the hunting season—mundane topics, yet strategic. I knew he was evaluating me. We didn't really know each other yet, and he wanted to check me out before talking about his life. Plus, there was the confidentiality factor: police are cautious before seeking advice about their affair with the waitress at the all-night café. What they say might show up on their service record in the personnel file, or worse, become departmental scuttlebutt. Officers often test a chaplain's confidentiality by sharing a tidbit of data and seeing whether it pops up as gossip around the station. Once satisfied with a chaplain's basic competence, view of life, and capacity to keep secrets, the officer will establish a bond of trust with him. A volunteer chaplain is the perfect one to confide in—a professional friend with whom they can talk informally outside the administrative chain of command.

And there is much to talk about. In our county, 70 percent of the officers' marriages end in divorce. Law enforcement jobs bring incredible stress; the officers regularly must deal with the dangerous, delusional, and defiant. They must constantly exhibit perfect restraint or they risk imperiling a criminal case. So, all too often, they dump the frustrations they can't vent on the job upon their families. Or they go to the other extreme and clam up, keeping everything to themselves and thus distancing their spouses. (The next time you see a police car driving by, thank God for the officer inside and pray for his or her family life.)

Anyway, given that background, you can see there was a lot going on that Sunday afternoon during my chat with the officer in his squad car. Suddenly, our conversation was interrupted as the radio buzzed. Dispatch gave us a spine-chilling assignment. Somebody was trying to kidnap a little girl outside a Mexican restaurant. As I recall, it may have been a Code 3 situation for all available units—which means everybody gets there as soon as they safely can.

By the time we arrived, the sobbing child was secure in her mother's arms. Brave passersby had become citizen heroes, grabbing the suspect and pinning him down on the sidewalk until police came. When we got on scene, another officer already had the bad guy in custody. The little girl went safely home.

Someday, we too will be safely home with our heavenly Father. And He will have shown the universe that He was both merciful and just in taking us there to live with Him forever.

Questions for Reflection and Discussion

1. If God is truly sovereign, how much responsibility is His for earth's suffering?
2. What human dilemmas are resolved by Christ's death on the cross?
3. Which example of suffering in this world troubles you the most? Why?
4. Have you personally known someone who committed suicide? If so, how did you cope with its aftermath?
5. If you could ask God face-to-face just one question, what would it be?

Chapter Five

PREDISPOSED TO PARDON

"Would you go up to Tahoe National Forest—as quickly as you can?" My supervisor's voice was particularly urgent. "I've got a death notification for you. A young woman just lost her twin brother in a fatal accident. Twenty-one years old."

I jumped into my Prius and headed into the Sierras. The summer sun had already set on this Saturday night. Everything was dark as my headlights wound up the steep grade on I-80.

Finally reaching the summit, I exited the freeway and soon found myself on one of Tahoe's many unpaved roads. Tall pines bore silent witness to the ghastly scene around the corner. The treetops reflected pulsating red light before I rounded a bend and came upon the emergency vehicles. A tow truck blocked the road.

I had to stop and wait, so I used the downtime to get more facts. "What's the situation?" I asked the officer in command of the first responders. In doing a death notification, a chaplain tries to gather all possible information en route to the location. As soon as loved ones get past their initial shock, they want the facts.

The crash involved three young guys in a yellow Mustang. There was one fatality—someone in the back, not wearing his seat belt. The driver, already airlifted, had a broken neck. The front passenger suffered only an injured hand; he had crawled out of the wreck and run for help.

The victims were part of a group of twenty friends from San Diego. Most were college students; some served in the navy. They were enjoying a long July 4 weekend at one of the small lakes in the forest. Their day was spent swimming and canoeing. Just good clean fun.

Except for the drinking.

As the sun was setting, they left the lake and built a campfire. Hot dogs, junk food, and beer. Soon the alcohol was gone. Three guys volunteered for a beer run to the nearest town, ten miles away. They got several six-packs and hurried back to the party. The death car may not have been speeding. Besides, the driver was skilled from his training in the navy. But a curve in the road that should have been negotiated wasn't, and the Mustang slid off the edge. With no guardrails, it plunged down thirty feet into some trees.

Maybe the real reason for the crash was that the driver had been drinking. Not that he was certifiably drunk; just impaired enough to not make the turn.

Eventually, the tow truck let me past, and I drove to the campground a mile down the road. Word had already reached the dead man's sister. She was in the lodge, surrounded and supported by half a dozen friends.

I introduced myself. All she wanted from me was the answers to a couple questions and help finding a landline on which to phone her parents.

Where my services as a chaplain were most needed was back by the tents. The girlfriend of the driver had retreated there and was taking things very hard.

As the state police officer and I rounded the lake, everything was pitch dark and very quiet. Then we heard muffled sobbing. Our flashlight picked up figures huddled under blankets in the back of a pickup truck. As we approached, one of them asked, "Is my boyfriend OK?"

I told her he had a broken neck but he hadn't seemed paralyzed as they wheeled him into the helicopter. They had taken him to a valley hospital.

"Could you drive me there?"

I turned to the officer, who nodded.

I offered to have prayer with the group, and they gratefully accepted. We formed a dark circle and prayed for Jack, the one with the broken neck, and the sister of the deceased. Then Shari grabbed her purse and pillow, and we headed down the mountain.

"I hope he's OK," she said. "People die from broken necks."

I tried to offer what hope I could. "They told me his vital signs were stable. That's good news—plus the fact that he wasn't paralyzed."

Our cell phones were dead because we were in the mountains, so we couldn't call the hospital. It was a long hour-and-a-half drive through the middle of the night.

Shari felt the need to defend her friends. "Please don't think we just went there to drink. Nobody was drunk. Jack wasn't drunk. He's in the navy—he wouldn't drive drunk."

We talked a bit about God. I got the picture that the campers, though fundamentally decent people, were not particularly religious. How sad that church wasn't a compelling option for them.

Finally, we arrived at the medical center. Jack looked better than I warned Shari he might appear. Despite being medicated, he wanted to talk.

"I can't believe I killed my best friend."

I offered what comfort I could but couldn't deny what happened.

He was relieved to pray with me, along with his father and Shari.

Jack recovered. And then came a court martial.

I'm not sure how his case turned out. I'm sure the U.S. Navy gave him a fair trial—yet it was not quite the same as if he were an ancient Hebrew facing judgment.

A friendly trauma center

Back in Bible times, the justice system operated differently from those of American and Canadian societies and of all other Western cultures. Our judges and juries presume the innocence of the accused but remain strictly neutral. If they harbor a bias either for or against condemnation, our law demands their disqualification.

Not so in the Jewish culture. Hebrew legal code required judges to take the side of the defendant. Defending the accused was a duty so sacred that the judge refused to delegate it to a defense attorney. Instead, that was part of his duties. The *Jewish Encyclopedia* explains that "attorneys at law are unknown in Jewish law."[1] Hebrew legal code required judges to "lean always to the side of the defendant."[2] So, witnesses of the crime pressed charges, while the judge promoted the case of the defendant and was biased in favor of acquittal.[3]

Of course, the judge also had to execute justice. If evidence of the defendant's guilt could not be dismissed, he had to abandon his defense of that person and pronounce condemnation. But the whole Old Testament system was predisposed toward vindication.

This explains why David in the Psalms longed to experience the divine judgment: "Judge me, O LORD my God, according to thy righteousness; and let them not rejoice over me" (Psalm 35:24, KJV). Throughout the Old Testament, God's people found joy in His judgment: "A father of the fatherless, and a judge for the widows, is God in his holy habitation" (Psalm 68:5, KJV).

What would this have meant for Jack if he had been an ancient Jew?

Western courts presume that the accused is innocent, but in Bible times, the judge went even further. He would assume the proactively protective role that a defense attorney takes in our court system. In fact, the judge was required by law to harbor prejudice in favor of the defendant.

If there was a plaintiff pressing charges, Hebrew judges did maintain fairness for both parties. If the evidence obviously incriminated the defendant, the judge would abandon his defense and execute punishment.

So what does this mean for us in heaven's judgment?

God is prejudiced toward our vindication

God is on our side. " 'Do not fear, little flock, for it is your Father's good pleasure to give you the kingdom' " (Luke 12:32, NKJV). He is predisposed toward our salvation.

And there's more to this good news. In certain situations, the Hebrew judge appointed an advocate to assist him in defending the accused. For us, this Advocate is none other than Jesus Himself: "If anyone sins, we have an Advocate with the Father, Jesus Christ the righteous" (1 John 2:1, NKJV). He assists our heavenly Father by interceding for us as a defense attorney—our personal Priest: "Therefore, since we have a great high priest who has gone through the heavens, Jesus the Son of God, let us hold firmly to the faith we profess. For we do not have a high priest who is unable to sympathize with our weaknesses, but we have one who has been tempted in every way, just as we are—yet was without sin" (Hebrews 4:14, 15, NIV).

Yes, Jesus knows exactly what we are going through because He lived on this earth and suffered the same difficulties and setbacks that all of us go through.

Of course, Jesus never sinned, and that's a huge difference between His experience and ours. Another difference is that although He was totally innocent, as Son of man He bore the punishment deserved by all human beings. That's why "God made Christ, who never sinned, to be the offering for our sin, so that we could be made right with God through Christ" (2 Corinthians 5:21, NLT).

Wonderful news! Despite our good intentions, we are all full of sin, messing up constantly. Not Jesus. His life was always perfect. Yet He died as if He were a sinner—for our sake, so we don't have to die for our sins.

That happened two thousand years ago, on the cross. But Jesus didn't stay dead. He rose from the grave and went up to heaven as our Representative before God the Father. "Therefore he is able to save completely those who come to God through him, because he always lives to intercede for them" (Hebrews 7:25, NIV).

Do you realize that Jesus is busier up in heaven for us right now than when He lived on this earth? Here on this earth, He got tired as we do, needing rest and sleep. But now, He "always lives" for us—working literally 24/7, never sleeping and always watching out for us.

Countering our accuser

Why do we need Christ's constant attention? Because somebody's always out to get us. It's Satan. "Your enemy the devil prowls around like a roaring lion looking for someone to devour" (1 Peter 5:8, NIV). With his evil spirits, the devil continually tries to tempt us, harass us, and destroy us. Jesus is watching over us from heaven's sanctuary, working to keep us safe spiritually as well as physically.

The devil does something else after he tempts us—he accuses us in heaven's court of being guilty. The Bible calls him the " 'accuser of our brethren . . . who accuses them day and night before our God' " (Revelation 12:10).

Do you see the picture? Satan never stops accusing us. That's the bad news. The good news is that Jesus is continually defending us as our Priest in heaven's sanctuary, our Advocate with God the Father.

Let's look deeper into the Hebrew court system. According to the *Jewish Encyclopedia,* "In the nature of things some parties can not plead for themselves. Infants, boys under thirteen or girls under twelve, the deaf and dumb, and lunatics can plead only through a guardian; and it is the duty of the court to appoint a guardian for such, if they have none."[4]

How does this apply to us? Well, we are God's children. Just as kids depend upon human parents to protect and defend them, so we depend upon our heavenly Father. He appoints Jesus as our Advocate to protect us against the devil.

But what's this about being lunatics? Well, this describes us too, actually. We often behave insanely, treating worst the ones we love best, destroying ourselves with unwise relationships and other addictions, and polluting the world we live in. The Bible doesn't flatter human nature. "The whole head is sick" (Isaiah 1:5). Thank God we have an Advocate for our insanity.

There is another special situation in which the Jewish judge appointed an advocate for the accused. A husband would represent his wife and help the judge defend her if the charges involved her relationship with him.[5] The application today is that Jesus loves us as His people, just as a husband loves his wife (Ephesians 5:25). And just as a good husband would defend his wife to the death, Jesus actually did die for our salvation—and now He lives for us just as devotedly, serving as our Priest in heaven's sanctuary.

What if we are guilty?

You might be thinking, *This is all wonderful, but let's remember that the judge in Bible times had to be fair. In the face of convincing evidence against the accused, the judge had to abandon his defense and execute punishment. So where does that leave us, since we're guilty? It seems like the devil has a winning case against us.*

Not at all. God has all the evidence He needs—at the cross, where Jesus died for our sins. The very verse after the one that describes the devil as accusing us day and night reads, "They overcame him / by the blood of the Lamb / and by the word of their testimony" (Revelation 12:11, NIV).

So salvation isn't based upon our being good enough to make it through the judgment. It's about the blood of Jesus, which we claim as our righteousness. We confess our sinfulness and testify to God's grace for us in Jesus. In so doing, we overcome the devil's accusations against us.

This is such good news it's hard to get hold of. Victims of abuse seem to find it particularly difficult. Not only do the offenders steal the innocence of their victims, but often they also manipulate their victims into feeling responsible for the abuse.

For anyone who struggles with such false guilt, there is wonderful news from heaven's sanctuary. If we have entrusted our lives to Jesus, nobody has the right to condemn us. In fact, we don't even have the right to condemn ourselves.

Jesus' intercession for us doesn't mean He has to persuade His Father to be nice to sinners. God is already on our side. "Who shall bring a charge against God's elect? It is God who justifies" (Romans 8:33, NKJV).

So that's the good news from heaven's sanctuary. Jesus defeated Satan by His death and then triumphantly rose to life again. Now He defends us against the devil's futile accusations. As our High Priest, He works with our heavenly Father, who takes our side in the judgment.

Supermarket judgment

Back in the early 1980s, when I was struggling to learn this good news about the judgment and the sanctuary, a family experience helped me grasp it. This happened in the supermarket, of all places. I was standing in line with Darlene, my wife, and leaning on our grocery cart. Our kids found themselves utterly fascinated by the candy rack, hoping to persuade us to let them have an unscheduled treat.

First they tried the Milky Way bars. Nothing doing. Then the M&Ms. ("These have peanuts, and peanuts are good, Daddy, aren't they?") When that failed, they reached for the last resort, sugarless chewing gum. (You parents know what I'm talking about.)

As this was going on, a wonderful realization struck me. Here we were, lined up at the checkout counter without any doubts that the groceries would be ours—this despite the fact that there was a judgment of sorts to pass before we could take the goods home.

We couldn't just walk past the clerk and head out the door with our groceries. The clerk would decide if we were "worthy" of taking them.

What would she base her judgment on? The money in our hands. With cash to present the clerk, the groceries would unquestionably be ours. We could anticipate the judgment without fear because we had the money in our hands.

Heaven's judgment is something like that. Jesus is the Treasure we need to pass God's celestial checkout in the sanctuary. With Jesus, we can be assured of a favorable verdict, whatever our struggles may be. God isn't threatened by our faults and failures.

Just as those who own Safeway supermarkets have decided beforehand that whoever has money qualifies for groceries, so God has declared that everyone who is in Christ qualifies for heaven. Can you see it? The test of the judgment is not whether we are worthy in ourselves. Our own spiritual accomplishments neither qualify us nor threaten us in that judgment. The question is whether we belong to Christ. We choose our verdict in the judgment by identifying ourselves with Jesus instead of with the devil.

If we entrust ourselves to Jesus, we are assured of a favorable verdict in heaven's sanctuary. The Father Himself is on our side!

Questions for Reflection and Discussion

1. What—if anything—did you learn about the judgment from this chapter?
2. Is what sense are Christians judged in God's judgment?
3. If God is on our side in the judgment, why do we need Jesus as our Advocate?
4. If God must ultimately be just anyway, what does it matter that He is predisposed to pardon us?
5. Why do we often treat the worst the ones we love the most?

Chapter Six

PLEASE DON'T TAKE HIM TO JAIL

Outside a nightclub in a darkened car, we waited for the new millennium. "Expect trouble," the sergeant in charge warned the rookie cop with whom I was riding. Thousands of students on holiday break had swarmed to our lakeside resort community to celebrate Y2K. Keg parties were all the rage.

As midnight struck, dispatch radioed our unit. Some teens on the other side of town were having themselves a merry New Year. Running barefoot down the middle of a busy road, they were frightening passing drivers and endangering themselves.

As we headed over there, word got out that somebody had called the cops. Arriving at the scene, we found only one reveler remaining, obviously bewildered. She said the others had dispersed across a vacant lot.

Our red-and-blue lights flashed across her frightened face. When the handcuffs came out, she meekly accepted them.

During the five-minute ride to the station to book her, she expressed remorse. She wasn't in town to cause trouble but just to see her grandmother. The neighborhood kids had invited her to party with them and some other visiting students. As midnight approached, the indoor fun had spilled over into mischief in the streets. Then everybody ran, abandoning her to face the charges all of them deserved.

"This is the first time I've ever been in trouble," she insisted. She said she believed in God and sometimes attended church back home. I guessed she was a decent person whose good looks had attracted the attention of local rowdies.

"So where do you go from here?" I inquired. "What plans do you have for the new millennium?"

"Becoming a nurse, maybe."

I suggested that a quiet night in custody offered her the opportunity to evaluate God's purpose for her life. With His help, she could make this negative experience a stepping-stone into an adulthood of usefulness and fulfillment.

I didn't get to offer prayer. That's awkward and usually impossible during an arrest.

Actually, I wasn't sure this teenager deserved arrest. Maybe just a fatherly lecture while driving her back to Grandma would have been enough. But it wasn't my decision to make. Rule number one for law enforcement chaplains is never challenge what the officers are doing. They might ask advice from a veteran chaplain, but rarely do they do so. When in doubt, they call for backup from other officers. Mostly, they rely on their own excellent training and instincts. Chaplains are there to support their decisions, not to question them or to otherwise get in the way of justice. And never should they interfere with an arrest.

But one time I did.

Interceding for a shoplifter

It was before I knew better—predating my volunteer ministry as a chaplain. While visiting my mother in suburban Washington, D.C., I took my kids, five and six at the time, to a pharmacy. In the parking lot, we saw a police car straddling the curb outside the store, lights flashing. As we walked inside, we saw that a man was being arrested. My kids had never seen anything like this, except in a video. This was live action.

"Daddy, is he going to jail?"

"It seems like he is."

Now the kids really got excited.

"What did he do?"

"I guess they caught him stealing something."

Normally I'm a proponent of "reap what you sow; learn from your choices." But something about this guy touched my heart—maybe it was his slumping shoulders. Seized with unexpected boldness, I ventured to interfere with justice through some undeserved intercession.

"I'm really sorry you have to arrest this man."

The officer turned to me and stared. "Yeah, we're sorry too."

Pointing to the suspect, I said, "I think this man is sorry too. He looks that way to me."

The officer frowned.

Naively ignoring that warning, I addressed the thief, "Aren't you sorry you stole that stuff?"

"I sure am, man."

"See, he's sorry," I pled hopefully. "I'll bet he'll never shoplift anything again."

"He's right! I'll never steal anything again as long as I live!"

"Yeah, right!" the store manager's frown said sarcastically.

"Look," said the officer, righteously resisting the audacity of grace, "you're obstructing justice here."

I apologized, and the officer's voice softened. "I'm sure you mean well, sir, but I've got a job to do for this man," he said, nodding toward the manager. "He's the one pressing charges."

I saw my opportunity. "Say, would you drop charges if I take responsibility for what this guy did? Let me pay for whatever he stole."

The manager scowled in a swirl of irritation, consternation, and amazement. "This store has a systemwide policy of arresting all shoplifters." Then he paused and shrugged. "But I guess we can make an exception, if you're willing to pay for the merchandise."

I pulled out my wallet. "So how much do I owe you?"

"Let's make it seven dollars."

I handed over a five and two ones, and the manager took custody of the ransom.

"Can he go now?" I petitioned the officer.

"Well, if the manager is dropping charges, I've got no grounds to arrest him."

Case closed. The handcuffs came off, and I triumphantly headed for the exit, trailed by my kids and our new friend. As our circus of grace paraded past onlooking customers and employees, some seemed amused and others amazed.

Outside, the pardoned shoplifter stopped and turned toward me. "Hey, man! I can't believe what you did in there."

I told him God had done the same thing for him with his sins recorded in heaven—a much more serious situation than charges against him here on earth. He didn't seem captivated by the grace that set him free. He just wanted to depart the scene of his crime. With a grateful grin and final wave, he dashed around the corner into a trash-strewn alley. Watching in wonder, the policeman ducked into his cruiser, darkened his flashing lights, and rolled out of the parking lot.

Maybe the whole thing happened for his benefit.

Celestial intercession

Alone again with my kids, I walked them over to our Mazda and opened the door.

"Wow, Daddy," they exclaimed, "we never saw anything like that before. Why did you help that man? Didn't he deserve to go to jail?"

"He sure did. I guess I felt sorry for him. And I wanted to show you what we were talking about in worship the other day—how Jesus intercedes for us in heaven as our High Priest."

It was an expensive illustration. Seven dollars was a stretch for a struggling young family, particularly in 1983 dollars. But I could have paid a lot more for interfering with the arrest process—with my own arrest, actually. Only fifteen years later when, I was a chaplain, did I realize how outrageous was my breach of protocol. Police risk their lives when arresting a suspect, who might be armed or who might have comrades lurking nearby, ready to jump the officer.

But I was just a foolish young dad, so the officer spared me. And maybe he had other reasons too.

I don't know whether the criminal beneficiary of my intercession turned his life around. Probably not, judging by how he dismissed my spiritual explanation of his release. Yet we never know this side of heaven what good we've accomplished. Maybe someday, he reflected upon the radical grace he received and recognized a dim reflection of God's star-spangled salvation. I do know my kids learned a long-lasting lesson about the sanctuary. They witnessed intercession in action, as mercy triumphed over justice. It showed them a new dimension of what Jesus is doing for them in heaven.

Our connection with God

Jesus is our connection to God. That's what He does as our Intercessor in heaven's sanctuary.

How did He become qualified to do this? He became the Son of man while remaining the Son of God. As Son of God, He connects God with us. As Son of man, He represents us to God.

Let's get some background on why this is a life-and-death matter to us.

When God created human beings, He didn't make us robots. He equipped us with freedom of choice, just as the angels in heaven could decide whether to follow God or Lucifer.

Heaven's rebels were cast to this earth and granted opportunity to prove their claim that Lucifer offered a better government. This earth became the theater of the universe.

Along came Adam and Eve, created as God's children. Adam was "the son of God" (Luke 3:38). The devil targeted him because of this, knowing he could injure God by ruining that relationship. But he couldn't ruin it without Adam's cooperation—without Adam abusing his power of choice by choosing to separate from God and join the devil's rebellion. The tree of temptation was Adam's voting booth, where he decided whether or not to be faithful to God.

The stakes were high. God is life, and by cutting himself off from Him, Adam would be choosing death. So God warned, " 'in the day that you eat of it you shall surely die' " (Genesis 2:17, NKJV).

You know what happened next. No sooner did Adam and Eve align themselves with the devil than they lost everything, not only for themselves but also for the whole world—all nature, all animals, and the entire human race. They ruined it for all of us.

What gave Adam such power over us? He held that power because he was the father of humanity. The name *Adam* means "man," or "humanity." He was our representative. Our destiny was tied up in his choices—for good or evil, for better or worse, for life or death.

Death is the ultimate outcome of evil, as is evident all around us. And it all started with Adam, our first father.

Whatever fathers do affects their families. When dad is drunk, the family suffers his hangover. If he fools around and divorces Mom, the kids lose their Garden of Eden.

So when Adam sinned, it wasn't just for himself but for the whole world. He was like a bus driver, and all of us were on board with him. He twisted the steering wheel of his own free choice the wrong way, crashing the bus into the tree of temptation. That's how "sin came into the world through one man and death through sin, and so death spread to all men" (Romans 5:12).

Totally unfair! We never even had a choice of our own. Adam, our representative, wrecked our relationship with God and brought death to all humanity.

Christ's alternative humanity

Enter Jesus, humanity's new Representative. God so loved the world that He gave His Son to perish for all humanity, restoring everything we lost in Adam.

The Bible describes Jesus as another Adam (1 Corinthians 15:45)—Head of a new humanity. All of us died in the old Adam, and all of us died in the new Adam: "One has died for all; therefore all have died" (2 Corinthians 5:14). Jesus not only died *for* us, He died *as* us—as the Son of man, our Representative.

The old Adam died our death at a tree, in Eden. The new Adam also died our death at a tree, on Calvary. When the first Adam ate the fruit at

Eden's tree and tasted death for all humanity, he got us evicted from God's presence. But when the new Adam at Calvary's tree tasted "death for every one" (Hebrews 2:9), He restored us to God's presence. So the death of the new Adam succeeded for us after the first Adam's death had failed us.

Do you see it? Both Adams, who included us within themselves, brought death upon themselves. They died as our representatives, so as they died, we died with them. But our death in Jesus leaves us with a much different outcome than our death in Adam. "In Christ God was reconciling the world to himself" (2 Corinthians 5:19). The old Adam's death ruined our connection with God, but because of His resurrection from the dead, the new Adam's death restored that connection.

"Since, then, you have been raised with Christ, set your hearts on things above, where Christ is seated at the right hand of God. Set your minds on things above, not on earthly things. For you died, and your life is now hidden with Christ in God" (Colossians 3:1–3, NIV).

When did we die? When Jesus died. When were we raised from that death? At His resurrection. God "raised us up with Christ and seated us with him in the heavenly realms in Christ Jesus" (Ephesians 2:6, NIV).

It's amazing and also true: Jesus has brought our new humanity into heaven. By faith, "our citizenship is in heaven" (Philippians 3:20, NIV), where Jesus represents us as our High Priest—even as we represent Him on earth as His ambassadors (2 Corinthians 5:20).

In Adam's old humanity, we were cast out of God's presence—and we had no choice about that. But in Christ's new humanity, we are restored to God's presence. Both humanities are available to us. Our ultimate fate—eternal life or death—depends upon our choice between the two.

Accepting God's acceptance

Citizens of a free society choose their governmental leaders. In America, we have a House of Representatives in our nation's capitol. Their vote is our vote.

Now suppose we hear that they are voting for things we don't agree with, making decisions that bring us harm. The solution is simple: we vote for a new representative.

I think you see the point. As your representative, Adam cast a vote for death at the tree in the Garden of Eden. If you don't like that, you can vote him out of office in your life by choosing Jesus as your Representative. That's how you get saved.

Suppose, like lots of other people, you want to work for the White House. You prepare to prove yourself worthy of the job. You fill out an application and hope for an interview. When the FedEx driver pulls up to your house and hands you an envelope, you get excited. But not excited enough—you are merely hoping for an invitation to be interviewed, but what you pull out of the envelope is an actual job offer—from President Obama himself. He's even signed the contract, putting himself on the line for you.

Now you have a choice to make about whether you'll put yourself on the line for him. You'll never get your White House pass until you accept the president's offer.

Let's make this practical. Maybe you've thought that the way to be a Christian is to prove yourself a worthy person by successfully imitating the life of Christ. No, that's how to be a Buddhist or a Hindu. Millions of them respect Jesus as a worthy example and teacher of ethical principles—along with other notable gurus and ascended masters.

The good news of the gospel is not that God can turn you into a little Jesus to compete with the real Jesus. Imitating Christ is not how we become Christians. Accepting our identity in Christ is how we are born again.

I used to imagine that if I followed Jesus faithfully enough, God might one day, with eyebrows raised, grant me provisional status as a disciple. But when we read the Gospels, we discover that's not how Jesus got His disciples. He accepted them right up front. "Follow Me," He invited Peter, James, John, and the others. He drew them into His presence with full acceptance—despite all their shortcomings. The only uncertainty was whether they would choose to lay down their fishing nets and accept His acceptance.

Not everyone did. The rich young ruler was offered Christ's acceptance, but he rejected it and returned to the life he had been living.

Marriage illustrates salvation

There are many ways to illustrate the glorious reality of our acceptance in Christ. Consider how people get married. When I proposed to Darlene, she no longer had doubts about whether she was acceptable to me. But we weren't married yet. I had accepted her for my life partner, but she had a choice of her own to make. She had to accept my acceptance. Only then were we married.

After Jesus died and rose again as our Representative, God accepted Him into heaven. That was our acceptance. So, we don't have to worry about whether we're good enough to go to heaven. We're there already in Christ! But that doesn't mean we will go there physically when He comes again. We must accept our position in Christ. Only then are we born again into our new life with God.

Let's say that tomorrow a real estate agent knocks on your door all excited. Her client in a limo out on the street wants to buy your house for a million dollars. "Look at this! He's even signed the contract already!"

You could keep them waiting while you spent the day worrying about whether your house really was worth a million dollars or about what you could do to make it worthy of that appraisal. Or you could gratefully accept the offer and live out its benefits for the rest of your life, sharing unselfishly with those in need.

My friend reading these pages, God's salvation contract is extended to you in the nail-pierced hand of your High Priest, signed in the blood of Calvary. You will never be worthy of heaven, but it's yours right now if you will stop whatever you are doing and entrust your life to God.

It took me years as a Christian before I awakened to my status of being accepted in God's beloved Son (Ephesians 1:6). I was confused—like a young couple who came to America from Europe and joined our church. They decided to get married and asked me to perform the ceremony. After the usual pre-marriage counseling, I told them that they needed to get a marriage license. They did so immediately, several weeks before the event. I asked them to bring the license to me at the wedding rehearsal so I could sign it and mail it in. At the rehearsal, they handed me a manila envelope. When I opened it, I found inside not a marriage license but a notarized marriage certificate. They had been married—and hadn't realized it—God bless them! For the past couple of weeks, they had lived their lives separately, being careful not to kiss too enthusiastically so as not to invite temptation. They were hoping to get married soon, not realizing that they were already just as married as they could ever be.

We had the church wedding anyway, but the law of the land had already accepted them as married. Their part was to identify themselves with their certified status and continue in it day by day and year by year as long as they both shall live. As they moved in with each other, they would learn to live as married people.

It's already ours

Maybe you've heard about the boy who tried to buy the Washington Monument in Washington, D.C. He marched up to one of the national park police officers and offered a shiny quarter to buy the famous stone tower.

The officer smiled kindly. "Son, you can't buy the Washington Monument. In the first place, it's not for sale. And if it were, your quarter wouldn't be enough to pay for it. But the third reason I can't sell it to you is that you already own it."

"I do?" said the wide-eyed boy.

"That's right! Since you're a citizen of the United States, this monument already belongs to you!"

Such is our salvation in our Lord Jesus Christ. We can't buy it because it's not for sale. And if it were, our personal spiritual attainments wouldn't be worth a nickel toward paying for it—whether we are a shoplifter, a New Year's reveler, or the cops trying to arrest them. None of us is worthy of God's acceptance, yet it's already ours through the victorious accomplishments of our great High Priest.

In the next chapter, we'll explore this further.

Questions for Reflection and Discussion

1. What is the difference between imitating Christ and identifying with His accomplishments?
2. What does it mean to be citizens of heaven while ambassadors on earth?
3. What, if any difference, does the fact that Jesus is the Son of God make in your life?
4. What, if any difference, does the fact that Jesus is the Son of man make in your life?
5. What is your next step toward living a life more closely identified with Jesus?

Chapter Seven

DEATH AT THE TREE

A man phoned his estranged wife and said, "Look out the window and see the sunset. Isn't it beautiful? You'd better enjoy it because it's one of the last sunsets you'll ever see."

He wasn't joking. Several nights later, he broke into her home and murdered her and one of their teenage sons. Then he shot himself. Their surviving son witnessed the murder/suicide.

The call came in about 2:00 A.M. As I zipped my uniform jacket and grabbed my badge, I pleaded with God for wisdom. When I walked into the station, they took me to see Zach, just in from the murder scene. He was a normal-looking fifteen-year-old, except that the pajama top he wore was splashed red with fresh blood. My first task was to tell him he couldn't wash his hands, which also were covered with the blood of his mother and brother.

"Why?" he demanded.

I didn't want to tell him that because he was there when the shootings happened, the police had to consider the possibility that he had killed his family and then blamed his father—who wasn't alive to defend himself. The instincts of the police officers were that Zach was telling the truth, but they needed forensic evidence beyond his testimony to clear him.

To avoid explaining all that, I simply told Zach that the police were trying to support him by doing everything they could to investigate the tragedy. They wanted to establish his innocence for the record by doing a gunshot residue test on his hands. Then he could wash them.

"They don't think I did it, do they?"

"No, they don't," I assured him. "But they have to run the test anyway, in order to do their job. They have a list of things they always have to do, and this is one of them. It's quick—just swabbing your skin. They're ready to do it right now, and then you can wash your hands."

"OK," he agreed.

After the detective came in and did the test, Zach headed to the restroom as I waited, silently praying for grace to connect with this poor kid. When he came back, we sat together silently for a while, staring at the wall. He buried his head in his hands, overwhelmed with shock at the loss of his mother, father, and younger brother.

Zach obviously didn't feel like talking. But the detectives had some important questions for him, and one of the most important things chaplains do after a violent crime is to help traumatized witnesses calm down enough to be interrogated. They often have information vital to the investigation that they can't communicate while they are hysterical or too distraught to say anything. To get Zach to the point where he could talk to our detectives, I first had to get him to talk to me.

Some people talk about their feelings first and then about the facts. With Zach, as with many men, it was the other way around. First came the facts then some of the feelings.

I put my hand on Zach's forearm. He didn't flinch, so I kept it there.

"You were there when it happened, Zach?"

"Yeah."

Then, after a few more seconds of silence, the details tumbled out. "My brother Josh and I woke up hearing Mom shouting downstairs. It must have been midnight. Then we heard Dad's voice too, down in her bedroom. Josh and I ran downstairs. On the way, I grabbed the phone and dialed 9-1-1. Josh was a few steps in front of me as we headed for the bedroom.

"As Josh ran into the bedroom, he got shot first. Then Mom. I saw

Dad point the gun at his own head just as I got into the bedroom. He pulled the trigger on himself. Just three shots and that was it."

With bloodshot eyes, he turned to me and told me more.

"I ran to Mom. She was bleeding, but she was already dead. I tried to help Josh, but he was dead too. So was Dad. I was the only one alive when the cops came running in the door. They didn't let me stay at the house. They put me in a police car and made me come here."

Zach leaned his head on the interrogation table and quietly started sobbing. I leaned over next to him and put an arm around him, rubbing his shoulder. After a while, he settled down, like a baby being calmed. I motioned for the detective watching through the window to come in so he could get the information he needed. He jotted down a few notes and then left me alone with Zach again.

The longest night of Zach's young life ticked on, cruel and slow. "What's going to happen to me?" he wondered. "I'm all alone now."

"You're going to get lots of love from everybody you know. Friends at school. Teachers too. And if you have a church . . ."

I paused and he didn't respond to that. So I continued.

"Do you have relatives in town?"

He did. I asked if he wanted me make some phone calls. It was arranged for him to stay with an aunt, who by then had heard what had happened.

Outside, the first light was giving way to the dawn of a cold and cloudy day, the first day of the rest of Zach's life. Reporters waited outside the front door, eager for whatever we could tell them. "They're just trying to do their job," I told Zach. "You don't have to talk to them if you're not ready to. I'll be glad to do that if you want me to. I can take you out the back door to the parking lot. Your aunt will be waiting for you."

Before we went outside, I asked if he wanted me to pray for him. He did. Then he headed outside to the arms of his aunt. I was dispatched to the crime scene to talk to the reporters there and make sure nobody got inside the yellow tape now ringing the property.

All I was cleared to say initially was that there had been multiple fatalities in the home that night and that there would be a press conference later that morning. Neighbors and the community would scoop up every scrap of information, but information wouldn't solve anything. Three people had died in that house, and a young teenager had lost his whole family.

Death is the harshest fact of life. We all die sooner or later, but the way that Zach experienced the death of his family was tragic. Chaplains are trained to deal with such situations. It came to be something of a specialty for me. A sheriff's office dispatcher started calling me "the Buzzard," and the nickname spread among the various law enforcement agencies we served. (Amid the daily tragedies police confront, they often use morbid humor among themselves as a survival tool.) At a holiday banquet, they presented me with a framed cartoon image of a large scavenger bird and the words, "It's a coroner's case. Send for the Buzzard!" This document may not have the professional look of my ordination certificate, but it's even more meaningful to me in the ministry it signifies.

How was I able to survive and thrive in death situations? Because death is a defeated enemy. In almost taunting words, the New Testament declares, " 'O death, where is thy victory? / O death, where is thy sting?' . . . Thanks be to God, who gives us the victory through our Lord Jesus Christ" (1 Corinthians 15:55, 57). In the victorious name of Jesus, I could venture confidently into the domain of death and minister comfort to the living left behind. Later, if they were ready to hear it, I told them the story of how Christ conquered death on the cross and then, through His resurrection, introduced eternal life.

Let's do an autopsy of death and see how it met its demise through the victory of Jesus Christ.

Death is more than not breathing

We're back to the Garden of Eden. Remember, God had warned, " 'In the day that you eat of it you shall die' " (Genesis 2:17). Adam and Eve ate anyway. In what sense did they die since their hearts didn't stop beating?

Death is more than losing your pulse. Death is the demise of everything desirable, commendable, and valuable. Because sin is the opposite of love, trust, and justice; consequently, it is also an expression of death. Death from sin includes

- Alienation and isolation—death of relationships
- Selfishness—death of love
- Aimlessness—death of purpose
- Disease—death of physical health
- Dysfunction—death of emotional health
- Fear—death of hope
- Guilt—death of peace
- Shame—death of self-worth
- Pain—death of comfort
- Sorrow—death of joy
- Pollution—death of planetary health
- Bondage—death of freedom

All of this meant the death of what God had given Adam in creating him in His own image. Sin's inherent dysfunction destroys and dehumanizes people and their communities—including the community of the saved, the church. We'll talk about God's sanctuary solution to that problem in the next chapter.

Picture Adam and Eve crouching in the bushes. Their relationship with God had died; otherwise, they wouldn't have been hiding. Their relationship with each other was ruined; they were fighting, blaming each other. All the problems we suffer in relationships today have roots in our death in Adam.

So something terrible happened to us in Adam—sin led to death. The good news is that something wonderful happened to us in Christ—He conquered death and brought us life.

Our victorious Hero

For humanity's various lifesaving agencies, from police to paramedics to firefighters, death is always a defeat. But the death of Jesus was a victory!

"Only by dying could he break the power of the devil, who had the power of death. Only in this way could he set free all who have lived their lives as slaves to the fear of dying" (Hebrews 2:14, 15, NLT).

Christ's mission on earth was to defeat the devil, disable his kingdom, and ultimately destroy him. "The reason the Son of God appeared was to destroy the works of the devil" (1 John 3:8). Christ's death was the culmination of a lifelong series of victories over the devil that began with His birth. Jealous King Herod determined to murder the Christ child, but an angel's warning saved His life and that of Mary and Joseph. The devil's murderous plan was defeated.

As a boy, Jesus refused to be diverted from the purpose of His mission. At age twelve, He declared, " 'I must be about My Father's business' " (Luke 2:49, NKJV). We know nothing of His next two decades except that He spent His teens and twenties in Nazareth, a difficult and tumultuous place even today. When the time had come for Christ to begin His mission as Messiah, He put away His carpentry tools and headed down to the Jordan River Valley to be baptized.

By His baptism, Jesus officially identified Himself with the human race as the anointed Son of man who would die and then rise again as the Representative of a redeemed race. And at that event, God, speaking from heaven, publicly witnessed to Jesus' divine Sonship.

Immediately after Jesus emerged from the water, the Spirit led Him to the wilderness for forty days of solitary preparation for His Messianic mission. There the devil confronted Him with three major temptations that covered the whole scope of human moral weakness. Jesus came away victorious.

Then Jesus launched His ministry in His hometown, proclaiming Himself as Liberator of a race held in satanic bondage. His longtime neighbors weren't impressed, and neither was the national religious establishment in Jerusalem. Jesus declared, " 'If the Son makes you free, you will be free indeed' " (John 8:36). They scoffed. "We've never been enslaved to anyone," they said, forgetting their exodus from bondage in Egypt and later captivity in Babylon.

Although Satan-inspired religious leaders refused to accept their Messiah, many of society's outcasts welcomed Him. The poor and oppressed received Him gladly, thus defeating the devil's attempt to shut down His ministry. By word and deed He confronted the evil powers, defeating them at every turn. He forgave tax cheaters and came to their parties. He reached out to prostitutes and restored their honor. He healed lepers, enlightened the blind, and even raised the dead.

One amazing defeat of the devil took place outside the mountain town of Nain. Traveling with His entourage of the curious and the committed, Jesus encountered a funeral procession. A few seconds with the victorious Liberator turned the death march into a parade of life.

Jesus never lost a battle with the devil. His own death on the cross, apparently a crushing defeat, was actually His strategic masterstroke of ultimate victory. With His dying breath He triumphantly proclaimed: " 'It is finished' " (John 19:30). After resting on the Sabbath to memorialize His finished work, He burst forth from the grave, validating His claim: " 'I am the resurrection and the life' " (John 11:25). The earth quaked, Jesus' enemies quivered in the dust, and He soared through the skies to receive His Father's welcome and acceptance on our behalf.

" 'I am the way, the truth, and the life,' " He declared (John 14:6, NKJV). " 'I came that they may have life, and have it abundantly' " (John 10:10). In our victorious new Adam comes the "restoration of all things" that sin through death had taken away after the first Adam's rebellion (Acts 3:21).

So it is that Jesus defeated the devil and "abolished death and brought life and immortality to light through the gospel" (2 Timothy 1:10). He also conquered every aspect of death that shows up today in sinful and dysfunctional behavior.

Shunning the world's legalism

Victory over sin has been a fearsome challenge and wearisome burden to misinformed saints throughout Christian history. The word *saint*, for example, was bestowed by the medieval church upon a select few who supposedly were supremely Christlike and Spirit-filled. That dogma endures today—not only in the Church of Rome but also in many Protestant denominations. But in the New Testament, *saint* simply signifies those who have set themselves apart from Adam's old humanity to embrace and live out their new identity in Christ.

This insight empowers us to overcome our addictions and dysfunctions, along with whatever else partakes of Adam's old humanity. "Where sin increased, grace abounded all the more, so that, as sin reigned in death, grace also might reign through righteousness to eternal life through Jesus Christ our Lord" (Romans 5:20, 21).

So, having died in Christ's death and risen in His resurrection, "put to death therefore what is earthly in you: fornication, impurity, passion, evil desire, and covetousness, which is idolatry" (Colossians 3:4, 5). No longer need we escape our pain in addictions, for Jesus bore our sorrows to the cross, and now by grace we reign with Him. All this is possible when we identify ourselves with Christ's historic death and resurrection.

In setting us free from the power of sin within ourselves, our position in Christ also releases us from vulnerability to letting other people control our faith. Every church seems to have well-intentioned, strongly opinionated members who feel called to be spiritual Dr. Phils. They canonize their convictions on issues of diet and lifestyle, telling everyone what to do—sometimes even seizing control of a cowardly congregation and getting rid of uncooperative pastors.

This was going on in Paul's day too. His advice? "If with Christ you died to the elemental spirits of the universe, why do you live as if you still belonged to the world? Why do you submit to regulations, 'Do not handle, Do not taste, Do not touch' . . . according to human precepts and doctrines?" (Colossians 2:20–22).

Paul was saying: Remember that you died and were raised with Christ, so your life is not in this world. Then don't let the principles of the world control you. *"Worldliness" doesn't only mean fooling around with sin. It also names the other extreme—legalism, which is coercive rather than liberating.* People who control your conscience are of this world. "These have indeed an appearance of wisdom in promoting rigor of devotion and self-abasement and severity to the body, but they are of no value in checking the indulgence of the flesh" (Colossians 2:23).

Taliban religion comes on strong, but its strictures are useless in changing the heart. Terrorists of the testimonies may cast guilt and shame on bad health habits, but that doesn't help people trying to lose weight. They can scold us, but they can't transport us to heaven's sanctuary—the only place for grace to help in time of need. Human rules and self-help programs are a poor substitute for the power of Christ's resurrection, which is ours only when we embrace our victorious new humanity in Christ.

Goodbye to the old man

God's formula for victory over sin is so basic that we tend to overlook it: put off the old humanity, and put on the new. Such "truth is in Jesus: that you put off, concerning your former conduct, the old man which grows corrupt according to the deceitful lusts, and be renewed in the spirit of your mind, and that you put on the new man which was created according to God, in true righteousness and holiness" (Ephesians 4:21–24, NKJV).

Adam's old humanity is a dirty old man who makes us lust for sin. As one exasperated person put it, "Everything I want to do is either illegal, immoral, or fattening!" God's solution is not to argue with the old man of sin but to replace him with our new man—literally, our new humanity in Christ.

Most American and Canadian adults dearly want to lose weight. Many shame themselves, trying to resolve their food addiction and shape up.

Shame may feed a manic-style crash diet, but it starves a healthy, fulfilling lifestyle—which is the only sure way to solve weight problems, and many other maladies—permanently. Part of healthy living is hopeful thinking, and this we have in Christ alone: "May the God of hope fill you with all joy and peace as you trust in him, so that you may overflow with hope by the power of the Holy Spirit" (Romans 15:13, NIV).

Did you notice that the power of God's Holy Spirit is associated with hope, joy, and peace? People talk so much these days about the Holy

Spirit, but where is His power? Nowhere to be seen in our good intentions, fierce diets, and strict promises. Please carefully notice God's solution to this futility: as pardon for sin comes through the historic death of Jesus, so power over sin comes through the historic event of His resurrection. This is the basis on which we receive the Holy Spirit—not our feverish attempts to follow the right formulas *or even claim the right promises.* We can fast all day and scold ourselves in prayer all night, but which of us by taking anxious thought can add anything to our spiritual stature? " 'The joy of the LORD is your strength' " (Nehemiah 8:10).

There's no substitute for the real gospel. When we struggle with sin—whether overeating, pornography, an addiction to gossip, or timidity, and everything else—the solution is not trash talking about ourselves but reminding ourselves who we really are. We are sons and daughters of God through our new humanity in Jesus. This is the truth. It's even how we overcome lying: "Do not lie to one another, since you have put off the old man with his deeds, and have put on the new man who is renewed in knowledge according to the image of Him who created him, . . . Christ is all and in all" (Colossians 3:9–11, NKJV).

Living in Adam's old humanity is living a lie, because Jesus is "all in all" as our new Adam. So let us "put on the Lord Jesus Christ, and make no provision for the flesh, to gratify its desires" (Romans 13:14).

Inaugurating your own election

Do you see what's at stake? Both God's pardon and His power depend upon your choice between two competing humanities. Will you identify yourself with the first Adam by participating in his unbelief and rebellion against God's will? Or will you accept your liberating new identity in Jesus Christ?

The 2008 U.S. presidential election offers fascinating insight into how we exchange old Adam's humanity for new life in Jesus. On November 4, 2008, Barack Obama was elected by the American people to become the forty-fourth president of the United States. In December, the Electoral College made it official.

But Barack Obama wasn't president yet. He might have decided, after the long campaign, to remain the junior U.S. senator from Illinois. He had two identities to choose between, the old and the new.

If he wanted to be president, Barack Obama had to forsake his old identity and lay his hand upon the Bible, personally activating his election. And so it happened on January 20, 2009. Suddenly, all the powers and privileges—and responsibilities—of the office became his personally.

So with us. God has elected us in Christ. This election is a historic reality, but it doesn't make us Christians. We have the choice of retaining our old humanity in Adam. But if we put our faith in Jesus Christ and inaugurate His election of us, all the privileges and responsibilities of our new humanity are activated. We have the presence of the Holy Spirit from Pentecost, which empowers us to shun the dysfunctions and addictions of Adam's fallen humanity—and to experience and share the love that is ours in Christ's new humanity.

What's next? Just as Jesus was baptized into our humanity to officially become the Son of man, so we need to be baptized into His new humanity as a child of God. Baptism, like marriage, is the outward expression of an inward decision.

Since I've shared personal information about myself with you in these pages, may I now ask you a personal question? It's important. Have you been baptized? If not, I pray that all the good news we've discussed in this chapter will motivate you to pray about it. Then speak with your pastor. Nothing in your life is more important, or more wonderful, than to take your place in the Son.

Questions for Reflection and Discussion

1. If Zach, who lost his whole family, asked how he might benefit from attending your local church as it is right now, what would you tell him?
2. With death prospering everywhere, how can we convince anyone that Jesus conquered death?
3. How is baptism an act of identification with Christ and thus

more than merely a matter of following His example?

4. Besides Christ's death and resurrection and His temptation in the desert, what experience in Christ's life most impresses you as a victory over Satan?

5. How has Jesus lived out a victory over the devil in your life recently?

Chapter Eight

SANCTUARY FOR THE SEXUALLY ABUSED

Calls past ten o'clock at night are bad news for law enforcement chaplains. Somebody's daughter was murdered in a dark corner of a nightclub parking lot. A teenager must be notified that Dad just died on I-80. A depressed off-duty policeman committed suicide, and his widow needs to make it through her first lonely night.

For me, this Wednesday night call was the worst I ever received as a chaplain. Janice phoned my office with allegations of sexual abuse by one of our chaplains, Joe. Her husband had a fatal heart attack several days previously, and my colleague was dispatched to comfort the widow. She said Joe rubbed her body inappropriately when he hugged her. She also said he said things a man shouldn't say to a woman who isn't his wife.

And her husband hadn't even been buried yet!

Late as it was, I arranged a visit with Janice. I found her not only grieving about her husband's death but deeply confused about her visit with Joe. Had she done something to encourage him to act that way? I assured Janice there was nothing she could have done to deserve the type of behavior she had told me about. Chaplains operate on a strict code of conduct, and what she had described was way out of line. Janice nodded in agreement, yet she seemed plagued by guilt one moment and outrage the next. Deeply traumatized, she moaned, "What should I do? What can I do?"

"I'll take care of this for you," I assured her. "I'll report what you told me to our supervisor tomorrow, and he'll guide you through this. He'll also discuss it with the chaplain."

"I don't want to get him into trouble," she protested. "He did seem like a nice man, but then . . ."

"That's not for you to worry about. Besides, you have a funeral to prepare for."

"Would you help me with that?" she asked.

I promised Janice I would guide her through the planning process and then conduct her husband's memorial service.

What a tragic situation: confusion, outrage, and guilt. I phoned Joe to let him know what I'd heard and that I had to report it. I urged him not to contact Janice again unless he had clearance from the supervisor.

"You don't believe the stuff she's saying, do you?" Joe asked, pleadingly.

"It's absolutely unlike anything I've seen in your behavior," I said. "I couldn't believe what I was hearing, Joe. But I couldn't disbelieve it either. You know it's not my job to determine your innocence or guilt. Our supervisor will conduct that inquiry."

I don't think Joe was pleased with me, but I did report what I heard. The supervisor then asked me to visit Janice with him and introduce him to her. When we visited her, he assured her of his concern and that he would conduct a thorough investigation.

I can't tell you what happened with this case because I was called to work in another part of the country before it was settled. It wouldn't have been possible or even appropriate for me to inquire about the case when I no longer carried the badge of that police force.

What a sad experience. Never in my life had I been involved with anything quite so traumatic as these charges against a colleague and friend.

Restorative empathy

Another friend of mine earned her doctorate at the Seminary at Princeton University. Her doctoral project involved helping women who suffered sexual abuse, usually from men who were domineering—often their incestuous fathers. Sometimes the abuser was a religious person who committed his crime in the name of God. All the women in my friend's study had abandoned organized religion, and most had given up a personal relationship with God. The goal of the project was to discover what might help them regain their trust in God and, perhaps, reconnect with the church.

As I recall, the study found that all of the women associated their heavenly Father with abusive male authority. My friend gathered them into small groups and studied with them how God the Father is revealed in the person of Jesus, the suffering Savior of victimized humanity. They talked about Christ on the cross becoming the ultimate victim, beaten and humiliated, and that the abuse He suffered enables Him to understand and empathize with those who suffer abuse today.

This view of God completely transformed these women and their concept of their Father in heaven. All of them received some measure of emotional and spiritual healing—some changing quite dramatically.

I volunteer for The Hope of Survivors, an organization that serves victims of clergy sexual abuse. Many have distanced themselves from church and God. Some have sought escape from their painful memories by developing various addictions, including dysfunctional relationships. Their lives have been devastated and in some cases nearly destroyed. Many are profoundly lonely. Often fellow church members, even close friends, sided with the abuser and ostracized the victim.

In ministering to these victims at our weekend conferences, we explain that the clergyman, as both a spiritual leader and professional caregiver, bears responsibility for any pastor-congregant relationship that becomes sexualized. Then we connect them to Jesus, who suffered physical, emotional, and spiritual abuse from clergy.

I take it a step further, showing that our Lord is no longer a victim of His abusers. He rose triumphantly as they cowered before His powerful presence. He soared in our humanity to heaven's sanctuary, where He now reigns over abusers, their enablers, and corrupt institutions. Soon He will return to this earth and take us to a new home where abuse will never happen. Meanwhile, as our loving and faithful High Priest, He protectively watches over us. He invites us to cast all our concerns and confusion upon Him as He intercedes for our needs. In heaven's sanctuary He feels our anguish, soothes our resentments, and calms our fears.

Our spiritual birthright

Healing from abuse happens as survivors embrace their new identity in Jesus, which is something like receiving the ancient Hebrew birthright. Great spiritual and material benefits belonged to the firstborn son through the birthright. He didn't need to earn it; it was his to claim and enjoy because of his position in the family.

If the firstborn didn't want the birthright, he could forfeit it as did Esau, "who sold his birthright for a single meal" (Hebrews 12:16). He pawned it to feed a ravishing hunger. Some pastors do the same today, sacrificing their holy calling for the sake of illicit cravings and power over female members.

Adam forfeited the birthright of the entire human race, but Jesus won it back. Now, just like the ancient Jewish firstborn, we are born with an inheritance that we don't have to work for—and couldn't earn even if we tried. So we don't have to reconcile ourselves to God or make peace with Him; Jesus Himself is our peace (Ephesians 2:14). Because we couldn't find our way to God, He found His way to us.

In Christ we belong to God, and He belongs to us. Jesus said, " 'Abide in me' " (John 15:4). He meant that we are to stay connected to Him, holding on to our birthright even when we get discouraged. As we choose to activate our birthright by believing this good news, we are born again, and God's Spirit seals our inheritance (Ephesians 1:13). Of course, if we choose to reject our birthright in Christ, we will definitely and eternally lose everything.

Receiving the birthright is all about embracing our identity in Jesus. I confess my own struggles with this. It's like I'm born with the birthright of an eagle but was raised to think of myself as a chicken. Even church people treated me like I belonged in God's barnyard. So I started pecking around for bits of grain to grow enough spiritually to impress God, trying to scurry around faster than everybody else. I also competed with other would-be chickens in order to improve my position in the pecking order. Scolding from others or from myself didn't solve my spiritual dysfunctions.

Even now when I know better, I still catch myself pecking around the barnyard floor as if I see myself as being a chicken when God wants us all to soar among the peaks of the spiritual Sierras. At those times I claim His promise: "They who wait for the LORD shall renew their strength, / they shall mount up with wings like eagles" (Isaiah 40:31).

This word *renew* should actually be translated "change." We change our strength from the flesh to the Spirit, from living out Adam's fallen nature to living out our spiritual birthright. This is how we finally rise above the abusive barnyard mentality some of us have grown up with.

All of this is enormously liberating to victims of sexual abuse. Cherishing their bond of empathy with the suffering Christ gives them a whole new view of their tender heavenly Father. They revel in their powerful and exalted position in the risen and victorious Jesus, soaring like eagles to His throne of grace in heaven's sanctuary. The power of Christ's resurrection is theirs as they align themselves with the Spirit of His new humanity. Now they can cope with and conquer their circumstances, never again to submit to an abuser.

It's all about identity

We who have suffered abuse need not find our identity in the evil inflicted upon us and thus regard ourselves as perpetual victims. The victim mentality belongs to the old Adam, who was cast out of the Garden of Eden and had a reason to feel sorry for himself. But we are in Christ, and in Him, welcomed into heaven itself. We can make our home in God's sanctuary at the throne of grace, a safe refuge from all abuse.

So there's no need for victim thinking. We are even more than mere survivors of abuse. We are victorious daughters and sons of God in solidarity with Jesus. It's all about identity, knowing who we are and who we are not.

I have to remind myself continually about who I am. I confess this is a deep and daily struggle for me. Every morning I must take quality time for Bible study to discover anew my identity in Jesus, and then, in prayer, apply what I have learned about every duty and dimension of my life.

Is it worth the effort that it takes to forsake my old chicken-pecking identity and soar in the Spirit to the sanctuary? Only in this way can I say to the old man of sin, "I am dead to you. I'm not your plaything or victim anymore. I am a child of God, alive in the resurrection of my Lord Jesus Christ."

How about you? Do you feel so messed up and broken, so violated yet so sinful, that you fear the damage others have done to you might never be healed or that you might never be forgiven for your own sins? Then flee for refuge to God's sanctuary and embrace your new and true identity in Jesus. You can do that right now.

Forgiving our debts

In Scripture, forgiveness is basically a financial word. I saw a man illustrate this several years ago. He said our guilt before God is like a debt we owe Him but can never pay. When God forgives us fully and freely through the gift of Jesus, we are no longer indebted to Him.

This man spoke passionately about the death and resurrection of Jesus and said that God is willing to forgive us and embrace us as His children. He summed up his talk by casually asking how many in the audience owed credit-card debt.

Nearly everybody raised a hand, sheepishly, reluctantly. He then asked if somebody there would like to come forward so he could personally pay off all their debt.

People looked at each other and smiled. The speaker had used many illustrations, and this was a particularly clever one. They didn't know, as I did, that he was a multimillionaire who really meant business. He wanted to provide a dramatic illustration of forgiveness that they could never forget—and he could well afford to do it.

The speaker persisted: "Is there anyone here that will come up here so I can personally write out a check and pay off all your debt?"

Finally, one woman halfway raised her hand.

The speaker called her forward. "So you would like me to pay off your credit-card debt as a symbol of God's forgiving grace?"

The woman nodded tenuously. "Well, sure."

"Consider it done!"

"What?"

"You're out of debt. I'm not kidding. See me right after the program, and I'll write a check for the total amount that you owe. However much that may be, I can afford it."

People finally got it. They only wished it hadn't taken them so long.

Questions for Reflection and Discussion

1. Why do many church members blame the victim of sexual abuse?
2. What significance does Christ's triumphant resurrection have for victims of abuse?
3. How does scolding oneself only contribute to spiritual failure?
4. How does embracing a new identity with Jesus deliver someone from a victim mentality?
5. In what ways must you learn to think like an eagle instead of a chicken?

Chapter Nine

SERVANTS OF THE SANCTUARY

Nobody should ever die alone, yet it happens all the time.

John, a veteran policeman who lived near my home, suffered a serious drinking problem. He kept quiet about it, afraid of losing his badge. One night fellow officers even caught him snoozing in his car with open beer bottles beside him. I'm not sure whether they reported him, but he managed to maintain both his job and his addiction.

However, at home, life was falling apart. John yelled at the kids and their friends, causing chaos and setting a bad example. As for his marriage, "for better or for worse" turned out be worse than imaginable or acceptable. Tough love was his wife's last resort. She warned John that if he came home drunk again, she wouldn't let him in the door.

He did, and she didn't.

Homeless now, John resorted to a thirty-five-dollar-a-night motel with a bright yellow sign that belied its bleak environment. Retreating to his private panic room, John lay on the bed to contemplate his future. He didn't bother to get between the sheets. About midnight, he sat up on the side of the bed, pulled out his service revolver, and shot a bullet through his tortured heart.

The gunshot announced John's death and put him beyond help. By the time I arrived, his body was gone and the room was empty. Too late for ministry, I knelt on the faded blue carpet, close to the small circle of congealing blood. Within reach of John's pillow and in plain sight was a Gideon Bible. John couldn't have missed seeing it when he entered the room and switched on the bedside lamp.

I reached for the Bible, flipping through its pages of printed notes offering help from God: verses for when you're lonely, verses for overcoming addictions, verses for coming to Christ. All of them bore testimony to God's love.

If only John had reached for that Bible instead of his pistol. That was a chilling thought. Then another possibility, even more haunting, suggested itself: Maybe John did reach for that Bible, scanned a few verses and put it down, hopeless as before.

For some who seek it, God's grace seems like candy on top of the fridge—tantalizing and desirable but far beyond reach of a toddler. Sometimes you need a friendly human boost to grasp the gift.

Bibles from the Gideons have encouraged and helped save thousands of souls over the decades. Thank God for that wonderful ministry. But sometimes people cry out for a word spoken by a human being to help them understand the Written Word.

Long ago an Ethiopian court official ventured to Jerusalem for worship. Heading home, he was reading a "Gideon Bible" from his hotel room but not getting its message. Heaven's sanctuary dispatched Philip the deacon, who had to run to connect with the rolling chariot. Out of breath, he panted, " 'Do you understand what you are reading?' " The ancient traveler replied, " 'How can I, unless some one guides me?' And he invited Philip to come up and sit with him" (Acts 8:30, 31).

Thank God for Philip the deacon and his Bible study on wheels. Too bad nobody was there for John the policeman as he ignored the Bible and grasped the gun.

I'm not blaming anybody. His wife had tried everything to save her husband and their kids. There was a Pentecostal church around the corner where I prayed every Thursday morning with the pastor, a fellow chaplain. Like Philip, we both would have hurried to the side of someone in crisis. In fact, we did it all the time. I just got there too late for John.

God alone can judge John, so I'm not blaming him for what he did in that lonely motel room. Nor am I excusing anything he did—either to his family through the years or to himself that last dark night. Obviously, help seemed too far away, even help from God.

That's what the Psalms of lament are about. They're the psalms that David composed when he felt forgotten by God and humanity. God's Spirit can raise those psalms from the printed page to inspire fainting souls with the same help He provided David three thousand years ago. But sometimes our minds are just too confused to get much out of ink on paper—even though it's the word of God in print. Sometimes we need the Word made flesh.

The living Word

That's what happened when Jesus walked this earth. In this weary wasteland, He came as the Fountain of God's living Word—refreshingly personal. Yahweh had talked to the world many times in various ways, but He wanted to communicate His love even more clearly. So, finally, He Himself came, up close and personal, in Jesus. The world has never been the same since "the Word became flesh and dwelt among us, full of grace and truth" (John 1:14).

It was our living, loving God who hiked the hills of Galilee, who slept on the lakeshore with snoring disciples, who kissed the tears of worried mothers and carried their gleeful children on shoulders muscled by hard labor. He showed skeptical fishermen how to catch human souls with love that was more than bait on a hook.

But it wasn't long before the world was fed up with the Living Bread from heaven. Only by a miracle did Jesus survive the wrath of organized religion long enough to be nailed naked to a cross. But He didn't let that happen before creating and commissioning an alternative spiritual community called the church.

Jesus didn't deploy the church to defeat nations with the sword, as did Muhammad—and as did Christian Crusaders brandishing a red cross on their armor. God's plan was to conquer human hearts by love, one by one. And then He took these scattered grace-based converts and united them into a new human race, the fellowship of the church.

Jesus is not our "personal" Savior. We can't have Him to ourselves or have Him by Himself. We either have Him together or we can't have Him at all.

Christian living is a team sport. You can play golf or tennis by yourself. Not so, baseball or football. If you're not willing to commit to a team, you'll never toss a touchdown no matter how far you can throw the ball.

So with Christianity. But somehow it's always been hard for Christ's followers to embrace togetherness as a fact of life. That's been true since the days of the desert hermits. They imagined themselves as God's holy loners, purifying themselves for His presence.

A legend of loneliness in early Christianity was Simeon Stylites. As a teenager, he left his flock to join a monastery. His pilgrimage drew him into total solitude. In a sand-swept wasteland, he climbed a nine-foot pillar and made himself at home at that top. There he lived the rest of his life, isolated and insulated from the world, finally dying atop a pillar fifty feet high.

Christianity in confusion put Stylites on a metaphoric pedestal. Delegations of believers sought his out-of-touch counsel, and after his death, a church council pronounced him a saint—the cities of Antioch and Constantinople competed for possession of his emaciated carcass. For the next six centuries, ascetics known as "pillar saints" followed his example by living away from the world and the community of the saved.

Stylites had mastered the discipline of solitude, which I fear some today still consider more important than loving interaction. But if you want to do business with Jesus, you can't escape a comprehensive connection with His body, the church. When rescuing us from the ravages of this doomed world, God's Spirit puts us in relationship—not just with Himself but with each another. The community we share is the substance of life in the Spirit. "The basic human unit is not the independent individual before God but the individual-in-community before God."[1]

We pass or fail heaven's judgment by whether or not we embrace the body of Christ, His new humanity, in place of Adam's fallen fraternity and Eve's selfish sorority. Christ's parable of the final judgment warns that we must be inclusive enough to share with others the blessings of our common salvation (Matthew 25:31–46).

So God calls us together, but not for the purpose of making church life a perpetual picnic to which are invited only good people who don't curse in front of our kids, suffer hangovers, or fornicate. Christian socializing can't be selfish. The church isn't a cruise ship but a lifeboat, with crew members on deck. We are the body of Christ—His hands and His heart. "The love of God is shed abroad in our hearts by the Holy Ghost" (Romans 5:5, KJV).

Church rescues a widow

Once in my chaplaincy, I saw the body of Christ come alive in the hour of death. Dispatch had sent me to a house where a man had died unexpectedly. Walking into the living room, I glanced around to see if this was a religious household. We were trained to do this so as never to impose the mention of God upon an irreligious family. I did see several Bibles around, so the people who lived there weren't atheists. And a church bulletin told me they were active Christians.

That was the testimony of the written word. Then came the living word.

The doorbell chimed as I was praying with the widow. People flocked inside—members of her church. They knew where to hang their coats, having been there many times when the family had hosted a small-group fellowship. Soon the place was swarming with brothers and sisters in Christ, who were hugging the widow and weeping with her. They didn't need me; I didn't have anything to do. When their pastor came, he didn't have anything to do either. So we sat together on the coach and witnessed a living love letter. Something the apostle Paul said came to mind: "You show that you are a letter from Christ" (2 Corinthians 3:3).

Organized religion at its best—organized for ministry.

A church full of priests

When those church members showed up to minster, they served under the "captain of their salvation" (Hebrews 2:10, KJV), the High Priest of heaven's sanctuary. Just before Jesus left this world, He prayed to His Father, " 'As you sent me into the world, so I have sent them into the world' " (John 17:18, NIV). This word *sent* is the same from which we get the word *apostle.* The church community is the apostle of Jesus, dispatched into the world to represent Him—in the same way that He had come to show us His Father.

Jesus is our High Priest, a term that implies other, lesser priests also minister here on earth. Protestants have known this as theological theory for the past five centuries; Martin Luther discovered that you don't have to enter a confessional and confess your sins to a human priest to get them forgiven. He thundered, in sound waves that rocked the world, that the whole church is Christ's priesthood.

But somehow the church, then and since, has been silent on the full meaning of this truth. Sure, we've talked about being a priesthood, but only half meaning it. We've mostly seen this doctrine as defensive, passive— basically a way to escape the blasphemy of kneeling before a fellow sinner in order to obtain what God offers freely in Christ.

But we commit another blasphemy when we make the priesthood an unemployed noun. It's more like an active verb. Priests don't just sit there—they *do* something. They are, we are, Christ's living, loving body—all of us together. And the body of Christ has no limbs frozen to stillness by inactivity.

Millions of Christians are praying to see the old Jewish temple rebuilt in Jerusalem, complete with a restored priesthood to resume the slaughter of animal sacrifices. The question must be asked: What about the full and final sacrifice of Christ's body on the cross?

God's vision for final events is different. His priesthood is not headquartered in old Jerusalem's temple but in New Jerusalem's celestial sanctuary, with representatives serving as a living temple all over this planet: "You are living stones that God is building into his spiritual temple. What's more, you are his holy priests. Through the mediation of Jesus Christ, you offer spiritual sacrifices that please God" (1 Peter 2:5, NLT).

Without such an active priesthood of all believers, another question deserves to be asked: What about the full and final sacrifice of Christ's body *in the world today*?

The heavenly sanctuary is Christ's great employment agency for His people—all of us. Our vacation from guilt and death is a vocation for ministry.

Priests are foreign ambassadors

So God's priests are not just passive parishioners. We are ambassadors for God, embodying His truth to a world lost in lies about Him. Priests are connectors. Just as Jesus connected us with the Father, so we now connect people to Him.

Something else about priesthood. It's not about having a good time in the Lord, although when we lose our lives for Christ's sake, we do find fulfillment, purpose, and joy in addition to suffering.

Life is unfair, especially for priests. We get stuck with other people's messes. As a chaplain forsakes a warm and safe bed because somebody got drunk and caused a fatal wreck on an icy road, we willingly deal with other people's consequences. In this we "bear one another's burdens, and so fulfil the law of Christ" (Galatians 6:2).

Here is the long-awaited answer to the question of the earth's first murderer: " 'Am I my brother's keeper?' " (Genesis 4:9). Yes! This does not make us our brothers' and sisters' messiah. We can't take responsibility for what other people do to hurt them or what they do to hurt themselves. In that sense, "each will have to bear his own load" (Galatians 6:5). But we can help them cope with their painful consequences and experience the loving hand of God.

Priesthood starts at home. God calls the father to be the priest of the family. In his absence, mother must serve that role.

Marriage also is an occasion for people to exercise the priesthood, each spouse serving the other. Honeymoon goose bumps don't last. Many waste their whole adult lives trying to regain that spark by dragging a spouse to every counselor in town—a spouse who manifests all the eagerness of a cat going to the vet.

Please understand, I value godly professional counselors and have benefited from them in my own marriage. But it's not about changing your spouse. It's about changing the only person that you can—yourself. "Through love serve one another" (Galatians 5:13, NKJV).

If you have no family, take a look around your workplace or classroom. It's a dog-eat-dog world out there, and many of your colleagues have been infected with human rabies. You are a priest representing the healing Jesus to people you interact with daily.

Many times we spend thousands of dollars making cold contacts in evangelism while ignoring precious lost souls with whom we interact forty long hours every week. Again, please understand. We should take advantage of doing mail-outs, starting Web sites and radio and TV ministries, and using every possible medium, including blogs, to communicate the gospel. Just remember John, the policeman who died alone with the Written Word by his side. When it comes to spreading the gospel, high-tech does the job only when accompanied by high-touch. Priesthood is all about God's healing touch.

State of the dead in Christ

Who we are is even more important than what we say, which is good for the workplace because we can't preach on the job. Most employees can't even be openly religious in the factory, office, or classroom. But we can show love, and that gets more attention than the lunch whistle.

People will wonder why we care about them. What makes us different? That's when we can say a few words for Jesus' sake, "with gentleness and respect" (1 Peter 3:15, NIV). That means we must not be insensitive or pretend that we know all the answers to questions that we ourselves will be asking angels throughout the millennium. The world doesn't need the Bible Answerman as much as it needs the Good Samaritan.

Yes, people do have questions they want answered, but more along the lines of "Where are some real live Christians around here?" instead of "Where are the dead in Christ?" They crave a living touch from God and wonder why churches seem more fascinated with their own petty rules than with Christ's golden rule. A church like that comes across as dead, so its neighbors already know the state of the dead. Death is a sleep, we point out. Too bad so many who claim to be Christ's followers are asleep in the pews.

What people really want to know is where the living saints are. Once they encounter God's Word made flesh today—the twenty-first-century version of the body of Christ—then they might become more curious about what the Written Word says. That's when you might be able to get a lunchtime study group going. And then it will be seen that events in a church facility are most effective when they can reap the harvest of what the priesthood is doing in the neighborhood.

Even worship services can be designed with seekers in mind. And the men don't all have to wear suits—the angels don't mind. Isn't it more important that we be nice than look so nice?

Do we want an expectation that Christians all have to dress up in fancy clothes to be a barrier to somebody's experience with the body of Christ? What is there in the life or teaching of Jesus that would make us think that way?

Just asking questions here. The answers may be simple, but they're not necessarily easy.

And while we're at it—what other congregational habits might reflect denominational comfort zones in our particular part of the world but have nothing to do with the teaching of Scripture or the calling of priests?

We expect people to change radically when they become disciples of Jesus—and so does God. Our new humanity generates new behavior. But baptism is only the beginning of the radical changes God wants us to make. Perhaps some of these changes can involve making our churches become a more palatable spiritual feast for our guests.

Stretching out of our comfort zone

One Saturday night I was doing a ride-along with a veteran sergeant. We checked a lakefront nightspot that college students flocked to. Since liquor was served there, all those who entered had to be twenty-one or older.

Local high-schoolers hung out near the nightclub, aimlessly wishing for the day when they could get inside where the action was. As this old sergeant and I walked past them, making sure nothing illegal was happening, he suddenly stopped, turned to me, and said, "All these kids! They're just waiting to get themselves into trouble. I'm not religious myself, but I know they really need church."

He looked back in their direction.

"Where are the churches? They should have something going for these kids. Some kind of community center to get them off the streets and have some safe, clean fun. Games, music, refreshments—you know."

He looked at me. "Your church should be doing something here for them."

Indeed, but what could I say? We weren't ready for such spiritual adventure. We weren't prepared to step outside our comfort zone and do anything so radical

Maybe that old cop didn't go to church, but he sure had a heavenly vision of what the body of Christ could be on earth.

Questions for Reflection and Discussion

1. What traditions in your local church might present a barrier to visiting seekers?
2. How can "high-tech" and "high-touch" synergize more effectively in your church?
3. What would change in marriage and in singles' romantic relationships if both partners regarded their relationship as a ministry opportunity?
4. Has the ministry of a loving Christian community ever helped you recover from a trauma?
5. What is the first name of someone at work who might be responsive to your loving witness as God's ambassador? If you're part of a group, you can pray for all the names mentioned.

Chapter Ten

YOU ARE CONNECTED

While driving to prayer meeting late one summer afternoon, I passed a group of young adults on the roadside. They were milling about, looking confused.

What was going on? An accident?

Looking closer, I noticed one of those white crosses. The people were crying and laying flowers beside the cross. They seemed like sheep without a shepherd.

I pulled over and walked toward them, showing my chaplain's badge. As I stood next to their cross, they gathered around me, seeming to want me to do something religious.

I did. I asked them to talk to me. I inquired about the person who had died. He was Stan, their motorcycle buddy. A good guy. Their leader.

A few days before, some of them had been riding with Stan, close behind him. A pickup truck missed a red light and struck Stan broadside. He died, bleeding, in their arms.

Recounting the tragedy, his friends cried anew. Big guys wept unashamedly and hugged me.

After they had each shared memories of Stan, they were quiet. I asked if they would like me to pray with them. They said they would, so right there, with cars going by, we linked arms in a circle around the cross and prayed.

Afterward, they told me Stan's body was at the funeral home. Tomorrow night would be the viewing. They invited me to show up. I said "Sure." Then they asked if I would conduct a little service there for Stan, just something simple, if it was OK with his parents.

The next night I sat with an older couple beside Stan's casket as they shared their memories. It was so sad—for them because they lost their son; for me because I hadn't heard a word from anyone about God.

Suddenly, that changed.

Stan's dad reported that a couple of weeks earlier, his son visited an uncle in Los Angeles. This man had invited Stan to go to church with him. Although Stan wasn't religious, he went along simply because he liked his uncle. But during the service, something happened. The sermon ended with an invitation for people to give their life to God, and Stan had done so.

Stan's dad shook his head. "I don't know what happened at that church, but I'll tell you this. For the past two weeks my son was a different person!"

I almost shouted, "Praise God!" right there in the funeral home. The man in the coffin before me was a brother in Christ. He died in Christ—all because of the witness of a faithful pastor in a godly church.

Stan learned the gospel from a pastor, but I doubt he would have gone to the church that night if the pastor himself had invited him. Stan had responded to the invitation of someone he knew and loved and trusted.

You're connected

Lately, lots of unchurched people are reconsidering their opposition to organized religion, because every other organization—in business, finance, government, you name it—seems to be failing them. The body of Christ is getting another look from some unlikely people. Opportunities for His priesthood abound.

You may not realize this, but your pastor probably envies the access you have to people, the opportunities you have for ministry. People are suspicious of clergy, and they're in a no-win situation. If the preacher is a charlatan, they say, "I knew it!" If the pastors live with integrity and propriety, well, aren't they supposed to anyway?

But the priesthood comprised of lay members isn't so disadvantaged. God can do more through your access to the world than you can imagine—more than you can ask or think. Don't sell yourself short as a priest!

Perhaps you feel intimidated by some of the chaplaincy adventures you are reading in this book, as if you could never deal with some of these situations. I confess that I also felt intimidated every time the phone rang with a new emergency. Although I found ride-alongs with officers exciting, sort of a live *COPS* show, I can't tell you how I dreaded those wake-up calls from the dispatcher. Totally inadequate, I would fall on my face before God for a few seconds before pulling on my uniform. En route to knocking on someone's door in the middle of the night to give a death notification, I begged God's Spirit to communicate wisdom, courage, and love through me. He never once failed me. Neither will He fail you in your priesthood.

Each of us has a unique calling, deserving of one another's admiration and respect. God's calling will stretch us and keep us challenged—and keep us on our knees!

Priesthood of suffering

There is something else we need to know about priesthood. Because life is unfair: *priests suffer*. But there's an upside to this downer: God uses our suffering to equip us to serve.

There's nothing as educational for priests as the seminary of suffering. Other training is important—chaplains receive ongoing rigorous education, as do all pastors, teachers, and other professionals. Smart churches also invest generously in lay training, sending lay leaders to seminars or at least providing them the latest high-quality study materials. All of this is vital, but nothing equips us for ministry as well as suffering does.

For one thing, priesthood at its best communicates empathy more than sympathy. The most effective helpers are those who know by experience what it means to hurt. The better we know pain, the better we can relieve it with God's healing love. "He comforts us in all our troubles so that we can comfort others. When they are troubled, we will be able to give them the same comfort God has given us. . . . Even when we are weighed down with troubles, it is for your comfort and salvation!" (2 Corinthians 1:4–6, NLT).

Our heavenly High Priest is no stranger to suffering. "While Jesus was here on earth, he offered prayers and pleadings, with a loud cry and tears, to the one who could rescue him from death. And God heard his prayers because of his deep reverence for God. Even though Jesus was God's Son, he learned obedience from the things he suffered. In this way, God qualified him as a perfect High Priest" (Hebrews 5:7–9, NLT). "Since he himself has gone through suffering and testing, he is able to help us when we are being tested" (Hebrews 2:18, NLT).

I think you see the point. Jesus became a man of sorrows by joining the human race, and we too are plunged into suffering when we are born into this world. But after we are born again into Christ's new humanity, all the pain we have suffered in our lives finally makes sense. There is purpose in pain because suffering equips us for ministry to fellow sufferers.

Understanding the benefit pain brings doesn't make it fun to suffer. If it did, it wouldn't be suffering! But through all the trauma of life, you can be confident that God is equipping you to minister in a way and at a level not possible without pain.

As a writer and speaker, I am comforted to know that—if nothing else—everything that happens to me can be turned into a teaching illustration.

We love to quote Romans 8:28, how God works everything for good. We remind each other that this promise is "to those who love God"— and thus to those who submit to His providences. But there's another condition in that promise. The text says that the promise is "to those who are the called according to His purpose" (NKJV). If you read a little further, you'll see that His purpose is to "conform us to the likeness of His Son" (see verse 29). Continue to read and you'll see that this character transformation requires suffering. But toward the end of the chapter, Paul assures us that no suffering can separate us from God's love. Instead, we are bonded even closer to Him through our pain.

That's the good news. The bad news is that suffering doesn't feel good—and it usually doesn't *seem* good, either. It seems unfair—and, by human standards, it is unfair. But remember, this whole idea of priesthood is unfair. Constantly, strategically unfair. Let's get used to it!

Priesthood shares God's life

So if you are suffering cancer, find somebody you can comfort who has that dreaded disease. If you find yourself in a hospice, that too is a place for ministry. I say this carefully, yet confidently: We need not be morbidly fearful of death when we remember that death lost its sting when Jesus defeated it.

In fact, did you know that Christ's resurrection guarantees our own resurrection? The Bible says, "Christ has been raised from the dead, the first fruits of those who have fallen asleep" (1 Corinthians 15:20). Those of you with fruit trees in your yard know that the earliest peach is the promise of more to come—more of the same harvest. So Christ's resurrection is the promise of our own to come. His is the firstfruits, phase one of our own resurrection. The gap of a couple thousand years means nothing to God, for whom a thousand years is like a day.

There is something else I've found quite comforting in my ministry. A woman whose husband died asked me how God was going to locate the dust that her husband would disintegrate into, so when Jesus comes He can pull it all together to return him to life. I had never thought about that, but an answer came to mind that she found helpful: The Bible says that our lives are hid with Christ in God. This means that our unique DNA pattern is stored in heaven—just as a computer file is stored on a hard drive. You can push a button and print out a unique document—one like no other one on the face of the earth. But suppose your spouse accidently puts that document in the fireplace and all that's left of it are ashes that now are mingled with a lot of other ashes.

No problem. Just go back to the computer to hit "Print," and you've got a duplicate of your unique document. Its uniqueness was not dependent upon the paper but upon the "DNA" safely stored in your computer.

Likewise with death and resurrection: God has no problem restoring you even if your present body dies and disintegrates into dust mingled with other graveyard dust. Your uniqueness is hid with Christ in God—not in your feeble, frail body. Your DNA is stored within the new humanity of your personal Priest in heaven's sanctuary, whose own resurrection is the promise of yours.

And just as you can take any blank paper and restore your unique document, He can take any generic dust and restore your unique self—body, soul, and spirit—at the resurrection. And this is exactly what He will do. In some wonderfully mysterious way on the day when He returns, Jesus will activate the DNA of every sleeping saint.

At Creation, God shared His breath and created one man from the dust. "Thus it is written, 'The first man Adam became a living being'; the last Adam became a life-giving spirit" (1 Corinthians 15:45). The Greek word translated "spirit" is the same word from which we get *breath*. At the resurrection, there will be a mass reenactment of Creation. Breath will go forth from Jesus into the dust of the earth, and millions of saints will be raised immortal.

And that will be our resurrection! When the trumpet sounds, Christ's victorious shout toward the earth will communicate life-giving breath containing the DNA of millions. The dust will give up its dead, all of them unique, just as the paper in your printer will bear the re-creation of something unique.

Instant insight

All this came in a flash to me when a grieving widow asked me a question while I was serving as her chaplain in the hour of death. You've probably discovered that *God can teach you more in one moment than you can figure out in a lifetime*—right on the spot, even as you are ministering. Every pastor has had this happen while preaching, and so has anyone who shares the Written Word as a living epistle of Christ. Of course, any such divine insights are no substitute for diligent training, research, and preparation. Sometimes God sends them just to affirm that what you are doing counts for something.

Good things come to those who share. If you've lost your house through foreclosure, consider it an opportunity to share any lessons you might have learned—plus how God is blessing you despite adversity. If you have been abused, you can share heart to heart another victim's intensely personal trauma. If you've lost a child, you are thereby equipped as an empathetic priest to share with someone in similar bereavement.

Let's conclude this introduction to priesthood with some good news. Whatever your pain, as a member of Christ's priesthood, you never suffer alone. Fellow priests serve each other. And even if no other human being reaches out to you, Jesus promises never to abandon you in pain. "He has said, 'I will never fail you nor forsake you.' Hence we can confidently say, / 'The Lord is my helper, / I will not be afraid; / what can man do to me?' " (Hebrews 13:5, 6).

Beyond everything else, we glorify God by endurance in suffering as we allow Him to use it in ministry on behalf of our great High Priest.

Questions for Reflection and Discussion

1. What is the deeper meaning of "good" in Romans 8:28, in which God makes a famous but much-misunderstood promise to make all things work out well?
2. How does a vision of one's priesthood bring purpose to one's pain?
3. How can your own individuality be enhanced by interacting with a diverse church family?
4. What advantages might you have over your pastor in connecting with spiritual seekers?
5. What are you suffering right now that God can use to equip you for more fruitful and fulfilling ministry?

Chapter Eleven

SUDDENLY NOTHING MATTERED

It was Saturday night, always a busy time for 9-1-1. Frank and Sue went out clubbing. Perhaps they drank too much, because when they arrived home, about midnight, they started yelling in each other's face. The fight was furious; neither was about to give in. Then suddenly, right in the middle of their curse-out contest, Frank dropped dead. The argument was over. Sue had won.

The marriage was over, too. In one failed heartbeat, Sue went from angry wife to grieving widow.

Somehow, amid her panic, she managed to phone for help. As paramedics wheeled Frank's shrouded body out the door, police escorted Sue, sobbing and screaming, to the station. Someone had died suddenly, and they needed to determine whether a crime had occurred.

All they got was hysteria. "Frank! Frank! I'm sorry! Dear God, I'm really sorry! I just want him back. Now!"

Instead of Frank, I walked in the door of the interrogation room. Talking soothingly to Sue, I lightly touched her forearm as male chaplains are trained to do. But she needed to be hugged, held like a mother holds a baby. Only a woman could do that.

So I told the detective in the hall that I needed dispatch to summon my secretary, Julie. She was a county-trained crisis responder, one of several women who worked with the chaplains. Julie had won the respect of the department by the way she helped a mother whose son drowned in a boating accident.

Julie arrived at about 2:30 A.M., chaplain's standard time. She cradled Sue in her arms, gently rocking her maternally. Soon the convulsive sobbing became quieter quivering, which gradually subsided. I slipped out of the room and told the detective that they would soon be able to interview Sue. My job was done for the night, thanks to Julie.

Sometimes, as they say, the right man for the job is a woman. All police agencies recognize that certain responsibilities are better managed by a woman's particular skills and intuition—a reality that some churches have been reluctant to recognize.

No single person has all the gifts that a community—whether a government agency, business corporation, or church family—needs to function well. That's why the Lord specified differing job descriptions within the priesthood of all believers. Thus, priesthood is a specialty ministry, uniquely tailored for every man, woman, and child in the church. Their varying gifts harmonize in a symphony of service.

Earlier, we saw that when God unites us to Himself through the Holy Spirit, He also joins us to each other in fellowship and ministry. In this context, let's consider how this New Testament priesthood functions.

Spiritual giving from heaven's sanctuary

Priesthood is all about spiritual gifts administered by our High Priest in heaven's sanctuary. The Bible says that "we, though many, are one body in Christ, and individually members one of another" (Romans 12:5). Sharing the same spiritual body of Jesus puts us in closer relation to each other than if we were mere physical brothers and sisters. The Holy Spirit lives inside us all, uniting our lives in Christ.

As individual members of Christ's body, we mingle interdependently, needing one another while maintaining our unique identity. So,

If the foot should say, "Because I am not a hand, I do not belong to the body," that would not make it any less a part of the body. And if the ear should say, "Because I am not an eye, I do not belong to the body," that would not make it any less a part of the body. If the whole body were an eye, where would be the sense of hearing? If the whole body were an ear, where would be the sense of smell? But as it is, God arranged the organs in the body, each one of them, as he chose (1 Corinthians 12:15–18).

Not everyone has the same spiritual gift, which keeps us humble and connected—not only with each other but with God. You see, spiritual gifts are more than labels God gives to Christians, more than even their calling. *Spiritual gifts are the moment-by-moment expression of God's living presence in our lives.*

Sometimes people say, "I have the gift of leadership," as if they are endowed with some spiritual ability through God's calling. Maybe they know the difference between the natural ability of a worldly leader and God's spiritual call—but do they understand that *a spiritual gift involves the real-time presence of the Spirit*? Without His continual infilling, they have no spiritual gift. They have a call to lead, but they aren't fulfilling that call unless they have the Spirit's daily gifting.

Let's explore this further. Many people are born leaders. "Simon Peter said, 'I'm going fishing.'

'We'll come, too,' they all said" (John 21:3, NLT). The other disciples naturally marched in Peter's parade.

Lots of secular politicians are Pied Pipers. This isn't spiritual leadership but natural influence and talent. However, when Peter was converted, God chose to gift him with leadership *in harmony with the talent he was naturally born with.* God often does this. The personality He gives us at birth and the experiences He provides in life often—but not always!—indicate how He intends to gift us spiritually. Now, even when a natural leader has a calling to be a spiritual leader, *that gift is active only if and when the person is filled with the Holy Spirit.* Otherwise, even Christian leaders function in the flesh rather than in faith, often becoming either bullies or smooth manipulators.

Too much of this abuse happens in churches. People know they have leadership ability, and they sense that God has called them to use it in ministry. So they claim this calling as their *spiritual* gift, when it isn't. It is their *calling* but not their gift unless they daily surrender it to God's Spirit. A spiritual gift is actually the gift of the Spirit expressing Himself in our unique ministry.

Serving that's not in the Spirit

I confess that I fight this battle all the time. I believe God has called me to communicate. I'm a natural, and have had some training as well. Back in grade school, I was co-editor of the student paper. I've been writing ever since (although I've yet to win a Pulitzer Prize!). I can be clever in turning thoughts into words, depending upon that natural ability. But this is not a spiritual gift. Not unless I am filled daily with God's presence can I communicate His life of power, wisdom, and love.

Financial giving is one of the spiritual gifts listed in the New Testament (Romans 12:8). To give something, most people have to earn it first—unless they are born wealthy. Some business people have a natural ability to turn most everything they touch to gold. I know a woman who bought a property on the California coast—a house on a lot and the vacant lot beside it. She sold the lot for as much as she had just paid for the whole property. In effect, she got the house free. Savvy business people do that sort of thing all the time. I admire them more than I should. Maybe the word isn't *admire* but *envy*!

But this businesswoman was different. She sensed a spiritual calling to giving, and she daily sought God's Spirit in her life. That made her unselfish. What did she do with her free house? She devoted it to ministry. Her natural abilities could have gotten her the house—with some providential help from God, perhaps. But only because she was a Spirit-filled priest could she manifest such supernatural generosity. Otherwise, she would have persuaded herself that what she earned was for herself instead of for God.

Many church members, I'm afraid, do the latter. That's what Ananias and Sapphira, that fatally greedy couple we read about in Acts 5, did. Both had a natural capacity to give and a spiritual calling to do so. But they obviously failed to live in the Spirit.

Jesus isn't playing games with us by calling us to the spiritual priesthood. Without the filling of the Spirit, we are not Christian leaders, teachers, helpers, or givers. We may be doing all of that, but only from natural talent and not as a spiritual gift. Though we may flatter ourselves that we are functioning faithfully in the body of Christ, we are just unemployed priests unfaithful to our calling—busy as can be, but all flurry, and no fruit.

If this is you, don't get discouraged. Allow the Lord to change you. He forgives us and turns us right-side up. His Spirit gifts us with repentance and then gifts us for spiritual ministry. The idea is this: "Yield yourselves to God as men who have been brought from death to life, and your members to God as instruments for righteousness" (Romans 6:13).

Receiving the Spirit

God has given His Spirit to comfort us and inspire us to fulfill His purpose, but I confess that the words *Holy Spirit* used to make me feel terribly guilty. I am so thankful that I finally discovered one of the most thrilling, unappreciated truths in all Scripture: how we receive the Holy Spirit.

We often yearn to be filled with the Holy Spirit, but without knowing how, when, and why He came to God's people in the first place. Although the Spirit has worked on earth ever since Creation, during Old Testament times, He functioned primarily in the background through specially anointed prophets and leaders.

Things are different now. In Jesus, we all have full and constant access to His Spirit.

This change began at Pentecost, fifty days after Christ's resurrection. He had risen from the dead as the Head of our new humanity and at Pentecost took His place of glory as our High Priest in heaven's sanctuary. Because of this event, we all have His Spirit to comfort us, guide us, and gift us for ministry.

Why did I suffer guilt regarding the Holy Spirit? It started with what I read in the Gospel of John: "Up to that time the Spirit had not been given, since Jesus had not yet been glorified" (John 7:39, NIV). I interpreted this to mean that the Holy Spirit could not be given to the disciples because Jesus was not sufficiently glorified *in their lives.* I took this as a personal rebuke, concluding that I wasn't experiencing much of the Holy Spirit because I wasn't glorifying Jesus enough. In desperation, I prayed that I would glorify God more so I could have more of His Spirit—*as if His Spirit were a quantity I could qualify myself for!*

How mistaken! This glorification for the Spirit was not about me or about something for me to accomplish. When Jesus said those words, He had not yet ascended to be glorified by God as our High Priest in heaven's sanctuary. Then came Pentecost, seven weeks and one day after His resurrection. *On that very day,* the church received the baptism of God's Holy Spirit.

But wasn't the church of one accord, and didn't this make them good enough to get the Holy Spirit? Yes, the church was in unprecedented unity, but this didn't qualify them to receive the Spirit. In fact, their unity itself was an evidence of their experience of the Spirit rather than of their own spiritual accomplishment.

Notice the connection Peter drew between Christ's glorification at God's throne and His gifting of the Spirit that day: "Being therefore exalted at the right hand of God, and having received from the Father the promise of the Holy Spirit, he has poured out this which you see and hear. . . . Let all the house of Israel therefore know assuredly that God has made him both Lord and Christ, this Jesus whom you crucified" (Acts 2:33, 36).

So the glory that brought the Spirit to the church was the glory of the risen Christ, not any supposed glory supplied by the disciples. Peter didn't say, "We finally learned to all get along together, and because of that God gave us the Holy Spirit." Neither did he say, "We prayed harder and harder, and finally we prayed hard enough the get the Holy Spirit!"

What did Peter say? "God glorified His Son at His right hand, and because of that, suddenly today we have the gift of the Holy Spirit."

A few days later, Peter and John, Spirit-filled, communicated healing to a lame man. Everybody was amazed. Peter said, "Don't look at us as if by our own power or godliness we healed this man. God glorified His Son, whom you killed but He raised from the dead. That's how we have the power through which this man was healed" (see Acts 4:9, 10).

Just knowing that God's Spirit can be mine not because I glorify Him enough in my life but because Jesus rose from the dead and was glorified in heaven has lifted a ton of guilt off of me. My life has never been the same since I understood this.

Facts of life in the Spirit

The timing of Christ's historic accomplishments explains it all. He died on the cross, providing us with a forgiveness that we are to claim for ourselves. He also arose in glory to become our High Priest in heaven's sanctuary on Pentecost—which made the Holy Spirit available for us to claim as a gift.

Understanding this opens for us the way to God's throne of grace. We would not dare think about forgiveness without the historic death of Jesus on the cross. Just as certainly, we cannot imagine being filled with God's Spirit outside of the resurrection of Jesus and His ascension to the sanctuary.

Somehow, we are slow to learn this. I just reviewed a book about the Holy Spirit that never once connected His gifting with Christ's resurrection. It put the whole burden on us for how much we are glorifying God. I pray for the day when we will all understand that God already has glorified His Son at Pentecost, and this is how the Spirit is ours today.

We trust Christ's death for sins forgiven, and just as surely we may trust His glorification for the gift of God's Spirit. This leaves us free to serve God without worrying how much we might need to be filled with the Spirit. We just joyously present ourselves to God and then trust Him to give us His Spirit according to His grace and according to our need. And He does!

Let's review these facts of life in the Holy Spirit:

- The *time* was Pentecost.
- The *place* was heaven's sanctuary.

- The *event* was the glorification of Jesus as High Priest.
- The *outcome* is the Spirit-gifting of His priesthood on earth.

As I noted a few pages back, for five hundred years Protestants have proclaimed themselves Christ's priesthood. Recently, they have begun to talk about spiritual gifts too. And now we know that heaven's sanctuary is God's human resource department and that this gifting is actually the Spirit Himself continually expressing Himself in the ministry of each individual priest. From heaven's sanctuary, God both calls us to priesthood and equips us with His Spirit to lead, to teach, to give, to heal, to show mercy and wisdom, and to serve with all His other gifts.

Gold is just sitting there

Among those gifts is that of leadership. Good leaders are always looking out for their people, not to keep them dependent upon the leaders but to help them discover their purpose in ministry.

I don't claim to be a good leader, but I've always tried to be aware of untapped treasure in the church. Informed pastors work from the assumption that no matter what they are doing, there's probably someone in the church who can do it better with the exception, perhaps, of preaching sermons. The best preaching comes out of years of college and seminary training along with practical ministry experience.

There's another, deeper reason for pastors to do the preaching most of the time. As God's appointed leaders of the congregation, pastors have the responsibility to keep their God-given vision before the congregation, applying it creatively in the context of biblical preaching. I quickly add that pastors must humbly remember that for their vision to be worth anything, the congregation must own it. Vision is not about "me" but "we." A mutually shared vision is a Spirit-filled treasure that takes hours of discussing, planning, and praying on the part of church leaders led by the pastor.

Other than visionary biblical preaching, just about everything else the pastor is doing can be entrusted to gifted lay people. There must be a deep investment in training, mentoring, and collaboration. All the investment in time and expense repays itself many times over for the church, not only in pastoral time saved but in lives changed and energized—and people touched by ministry, both within the church and the neighborhood community.

As leadership expert John Maxwell often says, in a takeoff on a famous rallying cry of the old California Gold Rush days, "There's gold in them thar pews!"

Julie's story

Remember Julie, the church secretary who comforted Sue when her husband died suddenly? Upon arriving as pastor, I saw that Julie's potential transcended her secretarial job description. I could trust her to make decisions that normally would be pastoral discretion. She became basically an unofficial administrative pastor. I don't remember her ever making a misjudgment—although it would have been fine if she had, because she would have acknowledged it and learned from it.

I also noticed that Julie had leadership ability—and that she was a Spirit-filled disciple. She had earned the church members' deep respect. Women, particularly, looked to her for wisdom, understanding, and inspiration. Soon she became the church's women's ministries leader.

Julie manifested calmness, compassion, and wisdom in crisis, a rare combination and a sure qualification for chaplaincy, except that the county required all chaplains to be ordained pastors. So I recommended her for training as a crisis counselor in support of the chaplains. Soon we worked together not only as paid employees in the church office but, occasionally, on a volunteer basis, for the various law enforcement agencies that operated in our county. Julie is now in the final stages of full chaplaincy training. From the day she committed her life to God for service, she has been as fully a minister of God as I am.

In their own unique ways, many others in our congregation discovered their gifts just as Julie did. I'll never forget how they blended their various personalities, backgrounds, and experiences into a symphony of service for the congregation and the community. It was my joy just to conduct the orchestra.

Can we all get along?

In Christ's ministry on earth, He brought together disciples from very different backgrounds and expected them to get along. He called Matthew, a tax collector who was despised by fellow Jews—and particularly by the Zealots, a fiercely nationalistic group—as an agent of Rome. Yet Jesus also invited Simon the Zealot to be a disciple! If Matthew wanted a relationship with Jesus, he had also to serve with Simon. If he couldn't deal with Simon, he couldn't have Jesus either. That was true of Simon too. Women were among those who literally followed Jesus as well, and treated with honor and respect as fellow servants of the Savior (Luke 8:2, 3).

Every church seems to have at least one troublesome personality, and so did Christ's eclectic collection of disciples. Judas was their treasurer. But if you didn't want to be around that crook and hypocrite, you couldn't have the company of Jesus.

Lots of people use the excuse of not wanting to be around hypocrites to justify their absence from church and from serving in the community of priests. But every time you visit Wal-Mart for toothpaste or tomatoes, you place yourself among hypocrites and shoplifters. We just have to live for God, love one another, and thus set an example of a better way of life.

It helps to remember that there's a little bit of Simon the Zealot and Matthew the tax collector in each of us—along with the impulsive Peter and even the hypocrite Judas. God patiently works with us individually and also in community with other priests. He expects us not only to put up with each other, but also to serve joyously together as priests.

Our different personalities and preferences can add interest to life in the church community. Somebody wants everybody to stay for a party after a meeting, while others want to go home and retire early, turning the electric blanket up to medium. We aren't photocopies of each other, and that's OK. It's more than merely tolerable—it's God's cherished plan for His priests.

Although we are all different, we are equally important. The Bible knows nothing of spiritual superstars. The great apostle Paul humbly described himself as a fellow servant. Peter, the preacher of Pentecost who had known Christ up close and personal, described himself as a "fellow elder" (1 Peter 5:1).

Now, the fact that everyone in the church is a fellow servant of Jesus doesn't mean there are no leaders. The church community commissioned Paul and Peter with authority, and they used it—not to overwhelm God's people but to empower them in ministry. They served by giving direction to the various ministries of which God had made them overseers.

Yes, there are lines of responsibility and authority, yet we all serve Jesus Christ Himself. He's the Cornerstone of heaven's sanctuary, God's great salvation center and activities agency.

No superstars or smoothies

In a religious cult, a megalomaniac leader may bully everybody else into submission. He may even assign his deluded disciples new names that reflect his vision for their life. Whatever God had in mind in creating that particular individual doesn't matter to the leader—he defines reality for earth and heaven. It's all about his supersized ego. The group becomes like a fruit smoothie, homogenized and flavored to please the leader.

By contrast, a healthy church community is a fruit salad. While all members synchronize with each other, they retain their God-given particularity. Individual identity finds meaning, purpose, and expression in serving with all the other priests in the ministry community.

Watch children visiting a nursing home. Their individuality and uniqueness are developed in mingling with those of a different generation. A woman in a roomful of men feels special—in the context of mutual respect within the body of Christ.

What's true for age and gender is also true of ethnicity. The community of priests is a festival of nations. In the church community, members of different nationalities and racial backgrounds who normally might not interact much become one body of priests while still maintaining their distinct ethnic heritage as a manifestation of their magnificent Creator. Anything one person may have more of than do the others—financially, manually, experientially, professionally, or otherwise—is at the service of the group to enhance its ministry of outreach to the larger community.

The cross-pollination of ministry spreads God's blessings everywhere.

Many spiritual benefits that God wants me to have won't be mine unless He can inspire you to serve me. There is music I won't enjoy unless you perform it for me. (God knows I can't perform it for myself!) As our High Priest expresses His spiritual giftedness through our various ministries, we serve one another while serving Him.

A few Sabbaths ago in our worship service, I saw a toddler pointing a half-empty nursing bottle excitedly toward the stained-glass window above us. The sun was shining through and illuminating the face of Jesus. Some unknown artist had brightened the worship experience of that babe in Christ.

Yes, the church needs its artists to show us Jesus. Our heavenly High Priest equally needs umbrella bearers and restroom servants.

The digital age opens up new doors for ministry by younger members. In many growing churches, formerly bored youth are excitedly engaged in the ministry of creative technology. They do everything digital that goes on in the church, from serving with the audio/visual system to designing posters for community events. Responsible adults mentor them administratively while learning from them technologically.

Smart pastors are realizing that sermons don't have to be a one-person show. Teens can illustrate them with PowerPoint slides and YouTube video clips. If what they produce is sometimes too animated, retired members don't withhold their affirmation and appreciation; they continue to be supportive. The older priests are too busy to complain anyway, because the pastor has them researching future sermon topics. He or she solicits their mature insights, synergizing them with the artistic talents of the youth.

These days, lone-ranger preachers are riding off into the sunset. I have a friend doing a doctoral project on team sermon production by members young and old, coordinated by the pastor. Nobody wants to skip church and miss a sermon they helped produce.

There is a deeper purpose in all this than meeting each other's needs in the body of Christ. It even goes beyond reaching out to the community. God's grand purpose is to perfect the congregation of the saints, to build up the body of Christ so "that he might present the church to himself in splendor, without spot or wrinkle or any such thing, that she might be holy and without blemish" (Ephesians 5:27). This is more than obsession with trinkets and trivia, more than purging pickles and pepper from fellowship dinners. This is the fulfillment of God's eternal purpose that together we reflect His image, which Satan has worked so viciously and effectively to destroy.

As the final crisis of the great controversy between good and evil looms, God is not teaching His people to stand alone. It's together that He wants us to stand and serve. There is nothing in heaven Satan hates more than the sanctuary, God's salvation and ministry headquarters. And there's nothing on earth that the devil fears more than God's community of living, loving priests.

What a calling!

What a challenge!

What an adventure!

Questions for Reflection and Discussion

1. What does the real-time presence of the Spirit have to do with a spiritual gift?
2. In what way must Jesus be glorified for God's Spirit to fill Jesus' disciples? (See John 7:39.)
3. How can youth and young adults have more opportunity to participate in your local church leadership?
4. Who (besides the pastor) in your church family does God use to minister significantly to you?
5. When have you failed to serve God by not being Spirit-filled?

Chapter Twelve

SHALOM OF THE FINAL REMNANT

"He was nothing but a worthless #$@%."

Not a comment normally heard in church, particularly during a funeral. But this was at the Salvation Army, the arms and doors of which are always open to unlikely candidates for God's kingdom.

Men who normally don't go to church listened as I eulogized Scottie, one of the regulars at our daily homeless ministry. His drinking buddies were scattered throughout the sanctuary. So were various clergy colleagues in the community, including a police chaplain who also ministered to the homeless.

I told the group that Scottie was of infinite value to God and to us. That's when Sam's drunk hollering interrupted the service. His comment was too loud to ignore.

Could it become a teaching moment?

Praying for that, I stepped around the pulpit and walked down the center aisle to where the commentator was slouched.

"Why would you say a thing like that?" I asked Sam, trying to sound kind yet in command of the situation.

His reply was immediate and even louder and more belligerent "because he was nothing but a drunk #$@%!"

This was getting worse. Out of the corner of my eye, I caught the face of our summer intern pastor. Her eyes were wide with shock. Teachers evidently hadn't warned her about such possibilities at a sacred service.

Sam's brazenness caught me unprepared as well. I needed God's Spirit in order to help me turn this distraction into an opportunity to portray salvation in Jesus. Praying silently, I pressed on.

"Would the fact that Scottie had a drinking problem make him any less precious to God—or to us?"

The snickering stopped. With Sam's help, I had raised a life-and-death question for many of them. The Spirit was on the verge of a breakthrough.

But Sam dodged the question by grumbling, "I don't believe in God."

Instantly the answer came. "Maybe you don't believe in God, Sam, but *God believes in you.*"

Sam was stunned. The grace of God hit home with him and a number of others that day in the sanctuary of the Salvation Army. What was stirring in their hearts was *shalom.*

Peace isn't passive

Shalom is loosely translated in the Old Testament as "peace," but the Hebrew word has a deeper, richer meaning than "peace" as we usually envision it. Christians typically think about peace more like Buddhists do than did the ancient Hebrews. Most of us view peace superficially and passively—the absence of negativities such as strife, guilt, shame, and anger. By contrast, the biblical shalom is positive, energetic, and proactive— the fulfilling of God's eternal purpose for this planet and for our churches. I believe it is the end product of the sanctuary, which God's final remnant will disseminate throughout the earth like the fragrance of the ointment with which Mary expressed her devotion to Jesus.

In all 236 verses where the word occurs in the Old Testament, *shalom* starts with one's personal relationship with God and ripples outward to include the whole world, including the environment.

Personal shalom with God. Shalom begins in the heart of each believer who discovers peace in God's forgiveness and acceptance. This is important—in fact, essential—if we are going to be peacemakers. Unless we experience God's peace personally, our every attempt to share it with others will end in dysfunction.

Shalom at home. Peace does no good to the world if it stays under the pine tree in my backyard where I sit with my Bible, happy in Jesus as my personal Savior. Shalom calls me back into the house where I argued with my wife, compelling me to seek peace there. Dads might even have to apologize to the kids—and why not?

Shalom to the church. Shalom extends beyond a peace with our biological kin to our faith family, so that we care deeply about our spiritual brothers and sisters—even if we understand the weekly lesson study differently and have opposing convictions regarding worship styles.

Shalom in the marketplace and classroom. Shalom is not satisfied with a weekly blessing at church. It ripples outward to the marketplace, so that we seek win-win business deals, not using us our expertise or advantages to exploit others. For students, shalom goes beyond not cheating in class. It might mean taking notes for those who are absent and even investing a little time tutoring those who are struggling academically.

Shalom to the whole world. Shalom extends beyond the marketplace and classroom to people with whom we would rather not associate. It includes your part of town and stretches over to the other side of the tracks, so that people at the Salvation Army would cry at your funeral. Shalom goes beyond "God bless America" or "God save the Queen" to "God bless Africa" and Iran—and even the terrorists who shout "Death to America!" We want them all to be saved and healed in body and soul.

Shalom to the animals. Shalom in Scripture is so expansive that it even goes beyond the human to the animal world. Ancient Jacob wanted shalom for the flock (Genesis 37:14). We too should care about God's non-human creatures, refusing to exploit them. This provides motivation beyond personal health issues for becoming vegetarian.

Shalom to the environment. Biblical peace extends even to insensate creation: "peace for the seed," so that the land will yield its produce (Zechariah 8:12, literally translated). This gives a doctrinal context for reaching out to the millions who are concerned about climate change.

Our Creator God is "green." He expects us to be responsible stewards of this world, polluted as it is, even as we anticipate His earth made new.

Jesus envisioned all of the above and nothing less when He pronounced, "Blessed are the shalom-makers, for they shall be called 'children of God' " (Matthew 5:9 as we might translate it).

Shalom explains why righteousness in the Old Testament does more than sugarcoat sin. Shalom loves enemies, feeds the hungry, visits the lonely, and seeks social justice. Shalom makes us priests on earth, following heaven's leadership from our great High Priest.

An AIDS opportunity

Basking in the aftermath of the Salvation Army breakthrough, I found myself wishing that such a thing would happen in our own church sanctuary. We gloried in the truth we proclaimed, but truth without grace is a lie. Truth with grace amounts to shalom.

God opened the door a few weeks later when a call came to my office.

Sonja called me. She had a twin brother, Jim, who was homosexual and who had contracted AIDS. Life was fading fast, and Jim wanted to come home to his churchgoing sister's family and die in peace. At the moment he was in a hospital in Sacramento. Sonja was wondering whether I would visit him and anoint him.

"Certainly, if he wants me to," I replied.

Jim did want me to. I explained that the anointing service would involve dedicating his life to Christ. I told him it wasn't a magic cure-all, but symbolized a willingness to submit to God's will in faith that He can and will heal, but only according to His timetable. For many, this will be at the final resurrection.

Jim agreed, so we set the time for his anointing. It would be the upcoming Sabbath, after our church service—the first occasion on which I could bring one of our elders to the hospital.

Walking into Jim's small room, we came face to face with half a dozen incredibly beautiful women. I wasn't expecting such an entourage at a gay man's bedside.

Who were they? They were Jim's hair-care customers. He had been their beauty consultant. Tearfully, they testified about his skill and grace in helping them discover their beauty and feel good about themselves.

So what should I do about the anointing service? Should I leave until they finished their visit and then come back to serve Jim? Anointing is usually a private family affair.

But maybe, I thought, this could be one of God's unexpected teaching moments. I asked Jim if he wanted us to postpone the anointing or proceed with it. He urged me to go ahead.

I explained to the women what was about to happen and invited them to stay if they wished or to wait in the hall for a few minutes while I conducted the service. All of them stayed and watched Jim give his life to God. He claimed both forgiveness of sin and healing of disease through the death and resurrection of Jesus.

Forgiveness always comes immediately upon confession of faith in Christ, but I repeated to Jim for the sake of our guests that healing comes in God's own time and way—sometimes immediately, sometimes gradually, but often not until the resurrection. Jim agreed to these terms and repeated after me the sinners' prayer. Then I anointed him. And Jim did receive a miracle of healing—not from AIDS but from guilt, shame, and alienation from God.

As Jim's life faded away in the weeks that followed, we spoke often of Christ and the glories of eternity with Him. Jim's sister transformed her home into a hospice, and his gay friends were always present at our discussions and prayers. I hugged them all without fear—gays and lesbians know the difference between a Christian embrace and the other kind. Jim especially seemed to appreciate the touch of someone beyond the homosexual subculture.

Gays in the church

Death came too soon. Sonja's family asked me to have the funeral. We could have held it in the Salvation Army church, but I thought perhaps our church would be willing to host Jim's gay and lesbian friends. I took the proposal to the elders, and they agreed that it was a fine opportunity for ministry.

So it was that the following Sabbath afternoon, a hundred or so homosexuals showed up at our church. Many members came too. I was so proud of them—they warmly invited our guests to follow them from the foyer into the sanctuary.

It was an incredible service. God opened the door for me to make the gospel relevant to our guests. (Perhaps some of our members needed to learn it as much as our visitors did.) I explained how all of us are born with spiritual AIDS that we have inherited from Adam. All of us are doomed with an incurable disease of the soul (Romans 7:24). God in His mercy sent us a Second Adam—a new corporate Representative—who overcame where our first father failed us. By Christ's life, death, and resurrection, a new humanity was born in the body of Christ (Ephesians 2:14–16). Through water baptism, we signify our transition from our AIDS experience in the old Adam to Christ's new human race, participating in the faith community of the church.

People seemed to get it. During the lunch that followed the funeral service, a number of gay visitors talked quite openly about God and their interest in knowing Him more. A lesbian recording artist seemed particularly interested. She gave me one of her CDs, which communicated a lot of pain and anger. I hope she got some help from our church.

That night about midnight, my phone rang. The caller was Jim's former domestic partner. Excitedly yet thoughtfully, he said he had never expected to experience God in the way he did at our church. He was wondering if maybe we could talk about it some more.

What Jim's friend had experienced in our sanctuary was shalom from Jesus, the "Prince of Shalom" (see Isaiah 9:6). The punishment that brings us shalom was upon Him (Isaiah 53:5). Such is the gospel of our peace with God through Jesus Christ.

Shalom of the final remnant

As we conclude our contemplations in this book, let's go far away and long ago, to that night outside Bethlehem. Thousands of bright angels shone upon awestruck, unsuspecting shepherds. Their message was shalom: "Glory to God in the highest, and on earth shalom, goodwill toward men!" (see Luke 2:14).

Near where the newborn Christ child lay was the city of Jerusalem, which had never lived up to the promise of its name, "City of Shalom." And except for a bit of time recorded in the book of Acts, the church that rose out of the ruins of old Jerusalem has likewise failed to experience or share shalom.

But finally, in earth's last days, a community of priests will arise under the leadership of their High Priest in heaven's sanctuary. These are the final remnant of God's saints throughout the ages. They will submit to shalom and share it throughout the earth. Finally, the work of God will be finished and the great controversy ended.

On schedule, the New Jerusalem will descend from heaven, and universal peace will reign on earth from that great sanctuary. God will dwell with His people forever.

Nothing matters more than preparing for that event. God help us all to be Spirit-filled priests who spread His presence through shalom—first in our families and churches, then to the marketplace, and ultimately, to the whole world.

Such is the message and the meaning of the sanctuary.

Questions for Reflection and Discussion

1. What is the difference between the English word *peace* and the Hebrew word *shalom*?
2. In what sense do we all have spiritual AIDS?
3. What does *shalom* have to do with understanding heaven's sanctuary?
4. Where is shalom now lacking in your life?
5. What part of the shalom in the New Jerusalem do you most look forward to?

ENDNOTES

Chapter 2: True Confession

1. Marketing Evaluations, Inc., http://www.qscores.com/pages/Template1/site11/30/default.aspx. Accessed Nov. 30, 2008.
2. *Wikipedia*, http://en.wikipedia.org/wiki/Q_score. Accessed Dec. 24, 2008.
3. Marketing Evaluations, Inc., http://www.qscores.com/pages/Template1/site11/32/default.aspx. Accessed Dec. 29, 2008.

Chapter 5: Packaged to Pardon

1. Isidore Singer, ed., *The Jewish Encyclopedia* (New York: Funk & Wagnalls, 1904), II:293.
2. Walter M. Chandler, *The Trial of Jesus* (New York: Empire Pub. Co., 1908), 1:153, 154.
3. See Taylor Bunch, *Behold the Man!* (Nashville: Southern Publishing, 1946), 64, 66.
4. *Jewish Encyclopedia*, X:204.
5. *Jewish Encyclopedia*, II:294.

Chapter 9: Servants of the Sanctuary

1. C. Norman Kraus, *The Community of the Spirit* (Scottsdale, Penn.: Herald, 1993), 28.

IF YOU APPRECIATED THIS BOOK, YOU'LL WANT TO READ THESE AS WELL.

The Lord's Prayer Through Primitive Eyes
Gottfried Oosterwal

"Nana [Friend], teach us to pray."

Oosterwal, who was studying the unwritten language of these seminomadic, Stone Age people in the dense tropical forests of New Guinea, meditated with them on the Lord's Prayer. Translating it wasn't easy.

How do you translate "the kingdom of God" for people who have no political structures? Or "our daily bread" for people who eke out an existence in the jungle on roots and grasses and an occasional fish, and who are constantly in danger of losing their battle for survival? For mission to be effective, the gospel must constantly be shaped to the needs, interests, and sensibilities of the recipients of the message. The meditations in this book from a beloved professor, and the many new insights from a rare culture, make this book unforgettable.

Paperback. ISBN 10: 0-8163-2307-0

Mayday Over the Arctic!
Dorothy N. Nelson

"My pilot friend Aubrey and I are flying at the very threshold of the Arctic Circle. We have experienced the failure of our one and only engine. We are plunging 1,000 feet per minute toward the frozen world below."

Don't miss this story of an extraordinary woman mission pilot. Hers is the moving story of one woman's discovery of expanding horizons and unlimited challenges. As a child, Dorothy Nelson, daughter of a Midwest preacher, had dreams of going to faraway islands as a flying missionary. Her dream came true when she received her pilot's license at the age of forty-five. She's been flying ever since.

Paperback. ISBN 10: 0-8163-2291-0

3 Ways to Order

1. Local—Adventist Book Center®
2. Call—1-800-765-6955
3. Shop—AdventistBookCenter.com